Rink

Stories from an Oregon Ice Arena

F. Michael Sheehan

CRESCENT RIDGE
PUBLISHERS

This non-fiction book intends to provide accurate information about the subject matter. However, ensuring all information provided is entirely accurate is not always possible. The author and publisher disclaim all liability for inaccuracies or omissions in connection with the use of this book.

Cover and Interior Design: KUHN Design Group | kuhndesigngroup.com

Cover photos courtesy of Cindy Jensen, Eddie LeRoy, Ben Strehle, Jeff Gibb, and The Rink Exchange

ISBN Hardcover: 979-8-9867903-1-2
ISBN Paperback: 979-8-9867903-2-9

Published by:

Crescent Ridge Oregon Publishers, Eugene, Oregon
http://www.crescentridgeconsulting.com/publisher

Printed in the United States of America
First Edition - 2023

Crescent Ridge Oregon Publishers is a division of Crescent Ridge Consulting LLC.

Have you ever been unhappy skating?

JACK FALLA:
Home Ice, Reflections on Backyard Rinks and Frozen Ponds.

ACKNOWLEDGMENTS

Many people have their fingerprints on this book. I am grateful for everyone's assistance, support, and willingness to share memories, photos, and memorabilia. Appendix A includes a complete list of contributors.

I want to express a special thank you to Ken Evans for his leadership and efforts to keep the rink open.

Also, I wish to convey my sincere appreciation to Daniel Gomez, Toshia Holden, Flint Donugchak, and the entire staff at the Rink Exchange for their dedication to maintaining and operating this cherished rink.

CONTENTS

PART IV: THIN ICE

PREFACE

The graying hockey players are doing what they do best: telling tales and drinking beer.

With stories floating above the scattered equipment on the locker room floor, one player suggests: "Someone should write this stuff down."

"Yeah, someone should write a book," says another, leaning against the cold wall in his sweat-drenched t-shirt.

"Maybe I'll write it," I offer sarcastically. With a Pabst Blue Ribbon in my hand and still wearing most of my uniform, I decided then and there to take on the project. This rink means a lot to a lot of people, and I am beginning to understand what it means to me.

I grew up a pond hockey player, skating throughout the Massachusetts winter. After school, we hustled to the frozen pond with our sticks and skates. One friend brought a puck, and two kids offered up their boots to serve as mock goalposts. We danced across the ice in pickup hockey games until the winter darkness descended upon us. It always came too quickly. My best friends and I quietly walked home, tired but elated, forging vivid memories that would remain forever.

Before moving back to Oregon, I sold my skates, confident that my hockey days were over. Suddenly, 18 years later, the miracle of Lane County's ice rink rocketed me to familiar feelings from the bright winter days of my youth. I joined the adult hockey league in the summer of 1990 and have skated every season since.

My experience is far from unique. The decision to build the rink led hundreds of figure skaters, hockey players, and speed skaters to rekindle passions assumed to be long gone.

Over the past year, I conducted numerous interviews and extensive research. Many people in Lane County have no idea about the ice rink in Eugene, let alone that the Oregon Ducks have a hockey team or that Tonya Harding, Apolo Ohno, and Scott Hamilton skated here. In addition to hockey and figure skating, the rink established a speed-skating club and a broomball association in its first decade.

Capturing the vast set of experiences has been both a joy and a challenge. While many stories are from the hockey community, I have worked to incorporate the experiences of other user groups wherever possible. Throughout the process, I have reached out to many people and am grateful for their assistance. Unfortunately, several key individuals have been challenging to locate, and others have passed away. Some of these tragically left us far too young. The fleeting nature of time has inspired me to gather the stories and preserve this meaningful slice of Lane County's history.

The book primarily focuses on the early years of the rink. However, it is still not possible to acknowledge all the individuals who played a significant role in shaping the ice arena's history. I have struggled with this along the way, and I'd like to apologize to those not mentioned. Every person who has spent time at the rink is a part of this story.

There are four parts to this book. The first section briefly overviews local skating and the battle to build a rink at the fairgrounds; the second is devoted to the arena's first year. Part three covers the rink's growth amid rising financial challenges, and the final section entails the efforts of the Eugene community to save the rink from demolition in 2011.

This rink holds a special place in the hearts of countless individuals. It has been an honor and a privilege to chronicle the history of this beloved building.

PROLOGUE

December 1989

B ob Carolan got the call he was expecting—a call he'd dreamed about since arriving in Oregon in 1979.

"Dr. Carolan, Dr. Abraham is on the line." his receptionist called into his office. She put Dick Abraham right through.

This was not a call to review a chest x-ray or lab results. It was not about patient care.

Hector Smith and Dick Abraham, (Photo courtesy of Mitch Boriskin)

"It's on," Dick said, "See you at 9:30 Friday morning."

Bob rushed home and pulled out a large green duffle bag from storage. Around town, 20 other men were gathering their antiquated equipment. A new skating rink was about to open at the Lane County Fairgrounds in Eugene, Oregon, and the first event would be a hockey game.

The staff planned to open at noon, but Dick Abraham had assembled an eclectic crew of hockey players for a 9:30 game. Bob Schauer was so excited he forgot to take the skate guards off his blades and fell flat on his back as soon as he stepped onto the ice, laughing all the way down. The tallest and oldest member of the group was Canadian bagpiper Hector Smith.

It was a game of "shinny," or pickup hockey, just like they played in their youth on New England ponds or outdoor Canadian rinks. Some had relatively new equipment with helmets, shoulder, shin, and elbow pads. Others skated with 1970s-era gear you might find in a small-town Canadian museum: brown-horsehair leather gloves; old pants covered in duct tape; steel tube skates; cups with white-tape waistbands; a straight stick or two. Many of the helmets looked like they were made of heavy cardboard. One thing is certain, however — everyone wore a broad smile.

On the rink's first day, there was no need for the brand-new scoreboard on the east wall for the score and time remaining in the period — no one was keeping score. Childhood memories flooded back and filled hearts with a familiar, long-forgotten glow. They were all from Cold Country, where hockey is king. It was like riding a bike, except these skaters had spent far more time on ice than any fair-weather contraption. For some, it had been 20-odd years since they had skated, but after the first few strides on the ice, it felt like yesterday. Soon they were skating backward, doing crossovers, and finding how easy it was to move the puck from side to side as they moved up the ice. It all felt so comfortable, so familiar... hands loosely gripping their sticks with well-worn hockey gloves. The sounds from the rink generated a tide of memories: steel blades carving into the ice and the bright thud of black rubber pucks hitting the boards. It was glorious to be on the ice again.

It felt like a miracle.

Ninety minutes after they first stepped onto the ice, the exhausted and sweaty players were changing out of their hockey gear as the general public filled the rink. There were smiles all around and dreams of hockey games to come. As Dick Abraham said, "If you've played hockey once, you never lose that feeling."

Little did they know that some of that game's participants would become lifelong friends — taking-trips-together friends, checking-in-when-someone-is-sick friends, giving-each-other-constant-shit friends, great friends who would still be drinking beers and laughing together three decades later.

Outside, the line for the first public skate snaked all the way out to 13th Avenue. Well over 300 people would skate that day. Many had their own skates — white figure skates, battered hockey skates, and one 66-year-old had his old speed skates all primed and ready to go. Others planned to rent skates, including a surprising number who had never ice skated. Rink manager Kim Brusegaard beamed joyfully, saying, "This place has endless potential."

On the ice, Cindy Jensen, a strong pairs skater in her youth, weaved flawlessly through the crowd in her bright figure skates. Skating director Kelly Bollenbaugh tracked her down and asked her on the spot to coach figure skating, thus beginning Cindy's 21-year career at the rink. Another skater on opening day was Eugene Thiessen, 62, a past president of the original Eugene Figure Skating Club (EFSC) in the 1940s. The new rink's soon-to-be first EFSC president, Carolyn Brown, floated effortlessly around the crowded rink. The ice was too packed for jumps or spins, but the sounds of her blades gently carving into the hard ice was thrilling enough. Her hometown had just opened an ice arena where she would be back to skating four to five times a week, just as she had growing up in the Bay Area. Glorious!

Many on the ice had little to no skating experience, but Barclay Brasted, who had played on a championship high school team in Minnesota, zipped through the crowd on his well-worn, black-and-brown hockey skates. Sid Magee tapped "Bark" on the shoulder and told him that an adult hockey league was forming. Wayne Shantz, a 51-year-old Thurston High School English teacher from Canada, had been looking forward to playing hockey again for a long time. He'd tell a newspaper reporter:

"It's exhilarating … I've waited and waited for this; it's just sad that it came so late."

Day One was a huge success. Figure skating championships, broomball games, hockey leagues, speed skating competitions, thrilling tournaments, and fabulous professional ice shows would follow.

The future looked bright on December 22, 1989 — one day after the winter solstice.

PART I

BEFORE THE RINK

1851–1989

*We were the hands that made the ice the old
fashion way with a tractor and blade.*

GENE THIESSEN,
1940s figure skater and member of the Redwings hockey team

*Eugene is ideally located geographically, and the league would look
favorably on a proposal from the area if they can build a rink.*

ED CHYNOWETH,
Western Hockey League President

THE COUNTY

Lane County, stretching from the Pacific Ocean to the Cascade Mountains, was established in 1851, with an area roughly equivalent to the entire state of Connecticut.

The first Lane County Agricultural Society Fair was held in September 1884. Each year, the county fair exhibited local agricultural products and livestock. A highly anticipated summer event, farm families would plan for

Rural Lane County Bridge (Original watercolor, Don Tucker)

1911 Lane County Fair (Photo courtesy of Lane County Historical Museum)

months to afford time off to attend. For these families, the annual fair was not only a community gathering but a time to learn about new technologies and developments in agricultural science.

In 1909, the fairgrounds found a permanent 53-acre home on West 13th Avenue near downtown Eugene. The county fair drew large, enthusiastic crowds every August. Operations were financially solid as the population of Lane County grew each year. The centerpiece of the grounds was the large wooden horse arena that would play a role in the history of Lane County Ice Arena.

Eugene Ice Arena

Well before the community considered building a rink at the Lane County Fairgrounds, Eugene had indoor ice skating.

The Eugene Ice Arena, located at 1850 West 6th Ave, was established in 1941 as a nonprofit. A set of wide arched-steel beams supported the wooden structure. Beneath the floor, a compressor cooled five miles of coils buried in the sand. It was like a giant refrigerator. There was no resurfacing equipment to clean the ice, but they made do. The rink's Ford Model A dragged a sharp blade to shave the surface, and then volunteer workers sprayed fresh water to produce a new sheet of smooth ice.

One arena regular was Gene Thiessen, an outstanding skater who performed as a barrel jumper at ice shows and a star on the Eugene Redwings hockey team.

> I worked at the old 1940s rink, passing out ice skates and stuff when I was 13. My friends and I would be at the rink all the time. We weren't running in the streets; that rink gave so many of us kids a wonderful advantage.

After his skating career, Thiessen became a motorcycle-racing legend, breaking two land-speed records at the Bonneville Salt Flats. He passed away in Eugene in 2021 at the age of 93.

George Korn and Geary Worth managed the arena. Worth was the principal of the River Road Elementary School and a supporter of youth activities. Korn, who also founded Willamette Pass Ski Area, became the first president of the Eugene Figure Skating Club. They brought professional ice shows to the area each summer and, in 1948, established the city's first hockey team, the Eugene Redwings.

There was plenty of free ice time for local kids and a pickup hockey game every New Year's Eve. Gene Thiessen and his pals could often be found around the arena, helping make ice and maintain the facility. They called themselves "rink rats."

While the Ice Arena was open, the

Gene Thiessen (Photo from 1946 Frozen Fantasies program)

Heidi Stenuf, Austrian Olympian (Photo from Frozen Fantasies 1946 program)

Eugene Figure Skating Club became an early United States Figure Skating Association (USFSA) member. The group put on sold-out ice shows each year in collaboration with the local Shriners. One year the shows raised $2,500 for the Crippled Children's Hospital in Portland.

Hedy Stenuf taught at Eugene summer sessions in 1945 and 1946. She began skating in Austria, and at the age of 11, she won the European Junior Championship. Stenuf represented Austria in the World Championships and the 1936 Olympics, held in the small Bavarian alpine village Garmisch-Parten-kirchen. She placed second in the 1939 World Championships, then trained in London for the 1940 Olympics, which would be canceled due to World War II. Eugene was fortunate to have such an internationally acclaimed skater as an instructor; Stenuf would also twice play the lead for their annual ice show.

In 1946, at the annual Polio Benefit ice show, the Portland Eagles of the Pacific Coast Hockey League split up their squad to play. The game, played on Valentine's Day before 750 enthralled fans, was likely the first organized hockey event in Lane County history.

Eugene Redwings

The Eugene Redwings, Lane County's first hockey team, was established at the Eugene Ice Arena in 1949. They finished first in the four-team Oregon Hockey League, including the Portland Blackhawks, the Corvallis Beavers, and the Salem Hornets. Every home game was a sellout, with over 700 raucous and enthusiastic fans.

The Salem Hornets played games at the Salem Ice Arena, which opened in 1940 at 610 North Capitol Street. The hockey team shared the ice with

Tom Gillespie, Frank Sauer, Dick Gillespie, Roger Newton, and Gene Thiessen (Photo 1949 *The Eugene Register-Guard*)

Ice Show at Eugene Ice Arena (Photo courtesy of Lane County Historical Museum)

the Salem Ice Frolics, a vibrant group of over 100 talented local amateur and professional ice skaters. The Hornets finished second in the league but were outclassed by the Eugene team every time they met head-to-head.

The Corvallis Beavers combined Oregon State students and local skaters into a competitive hockey team. The Beavers had one ringer, Canadian Bert McIntosh, who coached the team, and a few college students had played high school hockey in faraway states. They played their home games at the Corvallis Ice Palace, 901 Kings Road, which was too small for a regular game with six players. Instead, each team played with four skaters and a goalie on the small, crowded sheet of ice.

The Oregon Hockey League lasted only one season. The Redwings, Hornets, and Beavers dissolved as the local rinks began to close one after another.

In the spring of 1949, the city condemned the Eugene Ice Arena building. The wooden structure rotted from moisture and condensation; one corner of the rink began to sink into the damp ground, so maintaining a level sheet of ice was impossible. After nine successful years of operation and wonderful experiences for those involved, the arena closed its doors forever.

By the end of 1950, the Corvallis and Salem rinks closed as well, leaving Portland the only Oregon city with an ice arena.

ELDERS

Two individuals with community ties from the 1940s were the oldest hockey players in the early days of Lane County Ice.

Chuck Seldon

A graduate student, Chuck Seldon, became one of the Corvallis Beaver's defensemen soon after the season's opening. The local newspaper generally listed Seldon in the starting lineup but less frequently in the box score. His most impressive contribution was in the 11-10 upset victory over the Portland Blackhawks. The *Corvallis Gazette-Times* reported:

> Bob Beall netted the puck on a pass from Chuck Seldon at he 15:50 mark in the third period to break a 10-10 tie and bring the Corvallis victory.

Seldon would go on to become a fixture at Lane County Ice. However, his skating slowed down as he moved into his 80s. When it became clear that he should hang up his skates and bow out of the adult league, he would need some "encouragement."

Legend has it that Bob Carolan arrived in a gold Cadillac convertible at the rink and offered Seldon a ride. In a scene out of a classic gangster movie, Carolan explained that it would be best for everyone, including Seldon, for him to retire from the league. He reluctantly agreed, but would attend public skating sessions for years, holding on to his hockey stick with both hands for balance. Chuck loved to skate.

Hector

Hector Smith arrived a little too late.

As he searched the US for law schools, he hoped to find one in a town with a hockey rink. Eugene—home to the Ice Arena and the University of Oregon Law School—sounded perfect. Smith's only problem was that he didn't begin school until the fall of 1949—just a few months after the Eugene Ice

Hector Smith (Photo courtesy of Dave Parkhurst and the Eugene Highlanders)

Arena had abruptly closed its doors for good. Nevertheless, Hector remained in Eugene.

Smith grew up in Medicine Hat, Alberta; he began skating at age five. He would later serve in the Canadian Royal Canadian Navy during World War II and play for the Navy hockey team. After the war, he moved to Eugene to study law and, in 1953, founded the Eugene Highlanders Bagpipe Band—the official Oregon Governor's Foot Guard. In Canada, his Navy band played for King George V and King George VI; the Highlanders would welcome Senator John F. Kennedy to Eugene in 1958; and in 1980, the White House invited Smith to play in the ballroom for Ronald Reagan's inauguration.

Lawyer, bagpipe band founder, prankster, and senior hockey player,

Smith finally realized his dream 39 years later when the brand-new rink opened. At 65, Hector became the oldest player in the hockey league. He'd also become a fixture at the rink, playing in the adult league and coaching his youth team, Hector's Hornets. He told the local newspaper that he skated five times per week, a realistic estimate given his frequent drop-ins.

Hector was a joy to be around and play with as a teammate. At every hockey game, he kept his hydrating drink tucked away on the bench for his use only. I remember it being a tan Bota bag. Some players believe it was an actual flask, but most recall it as a water bottle wrapped in gray tape.

It quickly became known as "Hector's Nectar."

No one knew for sure what the nectar was; when asked for the ingredients, Hector would only flash a big bright smile between his graying beard and mustache. An oblivious and thirsty new player once found Hector's hidden water bottle and took a swig. One thing was certain—it was unlike any water he'd ever tasted.

Hector was not one to let the facts get in the way of a good story. He told Bob Welch of *The Register-Guard* that:

> My genes give me the vigor of a man 15-to-20 years younger. My bagpipe piping developed a large pulmonary and cardiovascular system, and that's why I've been able to play hockey this long.

The Hector Rule

As he moved into his late 70s, Hector's teams needed to do something about offsides. It was hard for Hector to skate back to the blue line quickly enough to allow teammates to carry the puck into the offensive zone. As a result, the league instituted an informal rule for play to continue if Hector headed toward the blue line. The only other player to be covered by the "Hector Rule" was Chuck Seldon. Older players fear the Hector Rule; most claim the day the rule applied to them would be the day they hang up their skates for good. No one wanted a ride in the Cadillac.

Between hockey and the Highlanders Band, Hector stayed a busy man.

One of his partners said he practiced law "from time to time." Hector and his bagpipes often appeared unexpectedly at bars, festivals, hockey rinks, and parties, delighting the crowd with his playing and presence.

Hector Smith continued to skate and remained pipe major for over 50 years until his death in 2008. At the time, he was the longest-running bagpipe major in North America and perhaps the world. His passing left a void at the rink that will never be filled.

THE FAIRGROUNDS

While Hector practiced law in the 1960s, the annual Lane County Fair was slowly drifting away from its agricultural roots. The counterculture of the '60s had moved north into Oregon with lifestyles, communes, and values that most long-term residents did not understand or trust. A rural-urban cultural divide grew across the county that would linger for decades.

Original horse arena circa 1960 (Photo courtesy of Cathy Jacksch)

Hippies versus farmers and loggers versus environmentalists foreshadowed a late-1980s riff between equestrians and ice rink enthusiasts.

The fabric of the annual summer fair was in flux. Its highlights were more around amusement rides and concerts by performers like Bob Seger, Jerry Garcia, Jimmy Buffett, and Tom Petty. In 1972, a young Dolly Parton went on stage at the fairgrounds arena, not feeling well. The crowd's three standing ovations touched her profoundly, and she wrote the song *Eugene, Oregon*, which remains one of her favorites (Appendix D).

The musicians performed at the 1930s-era horse arena, a grand structure located at the center of the fairgrounds. Unfortunately, by 1977 the all-wood building had become a fire hazard, and the Eugene Fire Marshal called its for demolition. Lane County voters approved a $5.9 million bond to construct a new convention center and horse arena the following November. Most of the community was thrilled. Restaurants, hotels, and stores were optimistic about the tourism the new buildings would bring. The equestrians, however, were unhappy with their new facility. The 1979 horse arena became controversial and opened discussions for changes at the fairgrounds.

As the county population grew and federal timber payments increased, Lane County's financial picture remained solid throughout the 1970s. The annual county fair flourished, and magazines frequently listed Eugene as one of the most livable cities in the US. When the national housing market crashed in the early 1980s, it hit some parts of the country harder than others. In Lane County, the bottom fell out of the wood-products industry. This was Timber Country, and the local economy depended heavily on the industry. The county was in a financial squeeze due to reduced timber reimbursements and a surprising decline in population.

In 1983, the Lane County Commissioners told the Fair Board that it would have to manage without any county support. The horse arena had been losing more money each year, and Lane County Fairgrounds Manager Steve McCulloch had to make changes. He was looking at all options.

The Western Hockey League

A professional minor league hockey team became a potential solution to the fair's financial challenges. In 1987, the owner of the Victoria, B.C. team of the Western Hockey League (WHL) contacted local officials. With only three franchises in the US, the Canadian-based league was looking to expand southward, and Eugene was one of eight cities in the running.

Western Hockey League

The Western Hockey League was one of three top-level minor leagues in North America. It was a stepping stone to the National Hockey League (NHL) for many young players. Though new minor league hockey franchises are not the most stable business ventures, Lane County showed interest.

Hockey is Canada's national sport. As recently as 1970, 96% of NHL players were Canadian born. In time, though, the NHL teams would expand to sunny states like Florida, California, Texas, and Nevada. Hockey was spreading southward, and interest in ice skating rinks — ignited by Olympic Figure Skating heroes like Peggy Fleming, Scott Hamilton, and Dorothy Hamill — was booming in the 1980s.

Yet, the Lane County Fairgrounds Arena Building was far from an ideal site. Fraser McCall, the WHL owner, later admitted: "It wasn't love at first sight." However, Steve McCulloch was enthusiastic about the potential and would champion the effort to gain approval to construct a new rink over the next two years.

Two hours north of Eugene, the Portland WHL Winterhawks played to large, enthusiastic fans at Portland's Memorial Coliseum. Brian Shaw, the Winterhawks general manager, would say in 1988: "I think the league will look very favorably on Eugene." The Winterhawks were successful, and more than 50 players moved on to play in the NHL in their first 12 years of operation.

The idea of a WHL team in Eugene might have seemed unrealistic, but there was a blueprint just a few hundred miles away. In Kennewick, Washington, a new franchise drew 5,500 enthusiasts per game, and residents bought 3,000 season tickets before the new arena's opening. The population of the Tri-Cities was significantly smaller than Lane County, and optimists believed that if the fairgrounds could build an ice arena, a WHL team would follow. However, the WHL president, Ed Chynoweth, told the local press:

> It's a straight chicken-and-egg thing. There's nothing for us to consider until Lane County has an arena suitable for playing.

PONDS AND PLASTIC

If you arrived in Eugene before 1990 packing an oversized bag stuffed with hockey equipment or a pair of bright white figure skates, you were going to be disappointed. There were rinks in the Portland area, including the world's first shopping center rink at the Lloyd Center. However, there was no rink at the Valley River Mall or anywhere else in Lane County.

Canadian towns of 12,000 would likely have a rink, and across the northern part of the United States, there were countless indoor or covered-outdoor skating rinks. One would guess that Eugene-Springfield would have an ice-skating rink or at least area ponds that would freeze over in the winter. After all, Eugene is farther north than five of the Original Six NHL teams: Boston, Chicago, Detroit, New York, and Toronto. Only the Montreal Canadiens skate on a home rink north of Eugene, Oregon.

Across Canada and the Northern US, parents would flood their backyards once the temperature fell below freezing. All they needed was a green garden hose and long sheets of heavy plastic that would likely suffocate their spring grass. Neighbors would marvel at the beautiful sheet of smooth ice and arrive with their dull skates for hot chocolate, beers, and laughter. Teenagers played late-night hockey games; married couples held hands, and figure skaters jumped and twirled.

Skating on a frozen pond or lake was even better. One could skate for miles, passing pockets of four-on-four hockey, high schoolers cracking the whip, and lone joyful skaters.

Amy Adams-Schauer grew up skating to school on a frozen lake at the edge of her family's yard in Michigan. On days when the cold winds blew away light snow, Amy and her siblings would glide across thick ice to the edge of a lagoon one mile away. There they would change into boots and swing their skates over their shoulders for the two-block walk to the back gate of their Wing Lake elementary school. Girls were required to wear skirts at school, and Amy had to wear thick woolen pants underneath to keep her legs warm and follow the school rule.

Being a girl meant she would have figure skates, but that did not stop her from playing outdoor hockey with her brothers throughout the winter. After a snowfall, the kids in the neighborhood would go down to clear a wide oval stretch of ice right in front of Amy's house. Her Dad had built two small wooden goals wrapped in chicken wire, and when placed at each end, they had their own hockey rink. Ever the tomboy, Amy could hold her own with her brothers and the neighborhood boys, even though she was the only one in figure skates. She and her husband, Bob, moved to Eugene in 1986 and quickly became involved in the effort to build an ice rink in their hometown.

Ponds in western Oregon rarely froze, and no one in Lane County ever considered building a backyard rink. Although most of the skaters arriving from the north and east came to love the Eugene area, something was missing; something lost from childhood they assumed was forever gone.

On the other side of the Cascade mountains, The Inn of the Seventh Mountain had an outdoor ice rink in the winter, and occasionally a hockey or broomball game would break out. The Inn, however, is a good three-hour drive from Eugene. The ponds at another resort, Sunriver, would often freeze beneath feet of dry central Oregon snow. Rich Hicks, who had grown up in North Dakota, purchased a Sun River home in the early 1970s and helped clear the snow so that he and his friends could ice skate. Rich longed to play ice hockey like he had as a teenager in Fargo, but no hockey sticks were available locally. He drove to Portland for a Trail Blazer game and returned with 12 gently used sticks purchased from the back room of a sporting goods store. Over the following two decades, joyous hockey games followed at Sun River for Rich and his lucky friends.

Local skaters were initially excited when an artificial ice rink opened in 1976 on the ground floor of an old car dealership in downtown Eugene. The rink looked real with boards, a red line, blue lines, and speakers hanging from rafters playing elevator music for the skaters. The surface consisted of a special rigid plastic sheeting and a gel lubricant. After a hockey stop, the gel was supposed to provide an ice-like spray. Dave Jensen played in a demonstration hockey game on the artificial ice, and the locals crushed a visiting team from Portland. "It turns out we had a tremendous amount of hockey talent here," Jensen said. Dave would become a leader in the effort to build the local ice rink and an active member of the early hockey community. The skating experience at this revolutionary plastic ice rink was dreadful, and the rink closed after less than one year of operation.

Hockey expats attempted to play without an available sheet of ice. Tim Birr, who grew up skating on the frozen Yellowstone River in Montana, fondly recalls floor hockey games in the basement of his University of Oregon (UO) dorm. Cottage Grove had a brief roller hockey league with fishing net strung on two-by-fours nailed together to resemble goals.

Terry Smith drove the 20 miles south each week to play on the gymnasium floor. He had been a Bay Bombers Roller Derby team member that toured the country and could often be seen on Saturday afternoon black and white TV throughout the 1960s. Smith played as a Jammer, the only team member who could score points, and carried his skating skills through roller hockey and into the first season of LAHA adult ice hockey, where he continued to play for over 30 years.

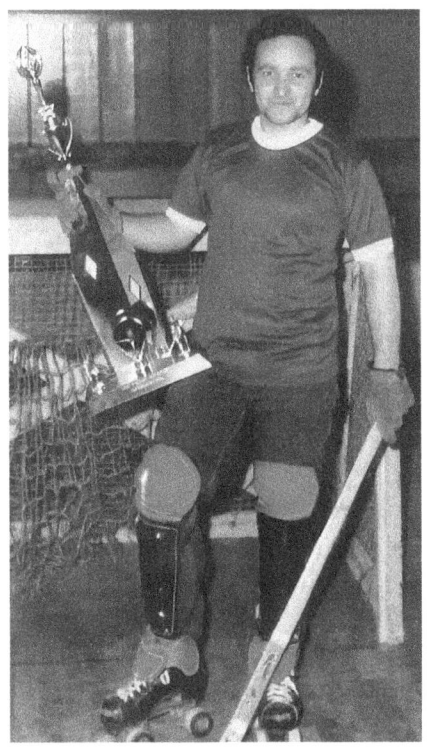

Terry Smith circa 1976

Floor hockey was available Thursday nights at Gerlinger Hall on the UO campus, but players had to put socks on their plastic stick blades so they wouldn't scuff up the gym's floor. It was the best they could do. Some had played top-notch hockey in their cold country hometowns and never discussed how deeply they missed the sport. Skating on plastic ice, roller hockey leagues, and games in a dark gym with socks covering their sticks were all far from ideal. In quiet desperation, they tried to find something that could briefly rekindle the distant feeling from their youth when they had real ice to play on.

Iced Days

Mother Nature would bring freezing temperatures to Eugene every few years, leaving passable ice for skating across Lane County.

I brought my ice skates when I first came to Eugene in 1972, and there were a few cold December days before returning to Boston for Christmas. A thin coat of ice covered the sidewalks, and I heard that someone was ice skating at the South Eugene tennis courts. For some reason, this was big news.

The next day I took a hockey stick and my skates to the courts, confident that others would soon follow for a glorious pickup hockey game. The ice was wavy, with plenty of cracks, but I could skate, and I was excited for my first game of the winter. A damp, cold wind settled on my long, curly black hair, making it stiff to the touch as I skated up and down the court, dribbling the puck with a roll of my wrists. When I approached one end of the frozen court, I fired the puck into the cold, gray chain-link fence. Clang!

To my dismay, I eventually realized no other hockey players would be showing up. Passers-by lingered for a few minutes to watch, and a 12-year-old asked if I was a professional hockey player. Two days later, I reluctantly packed my skates into a green suitcase for the flight back to New England.

When a thin pond behind the car dealerships on Goodpasture Island Road remained frozen for two bright December days in 1988, former amateur precision skater Dot Bloomfield jumped at the opportunity. Fellow figure skaters

Don Prebus and Helen Larson gleefully joined her on the ice. The three were core members of a growing skating enthusiast community who'd eventually convinced Lane County to build an ice rink at the fairgrounds.

Dot Bloomfield (Photo courtesy of Steve Hertzberg)

HORSE PEOPLE VS. ICE PEOPLE

Rumors of the WHL visit quietly spread, igniting interest for some in the community and fears for others. The plan was to convert the 4,000-seat horse arena into an ice-skating facility, much to the chagrin of the equestrian community.

For some, it was more than horses. Tensions between rural and urban Lane County had been quietly simmering for years. Some farmers and ranchers felt that the county fair was being cut off from its agricultural roots with a new focus on conventions and trade shows. Mutual distrust between fair officials and the agricultural community had been building since 1977, when the original horse arena was forced to close.

The equestrians considered the new 1979 livestock facility too small to hold even a decent rodeo. There were other issues. They built it on a concrete floor, and the dirt cover posed a danger for horses. The layout was problematic, and the equestrians were not pleased.

The horse arena building became a center of community controversy when the use of the facility plummeted. The number of events at the facility had dwindled from 38 in 1984 to just 17 four years later. The horse community blamed mismanagement and poor marketing. For whatever reason, usage declined, and the arena was losing approximately $50,000 annually.

Steve Hertzberg

A local high school teacher, Steve Hertzberg, heard that the fairgrounds was considering a new ice arena, so he attended an open board meeting in early 1988. His interest in hockey began at summer camp in rural Quebec, and when an ice rink opened in his Long Island hometown, he began playing pickup hockey. Steve attended the Massachusetts Institute of Technology (MIT), where he decided to try out for the freshman hockey team. Fortunately, if you went out for the team at MIT, you made the team.

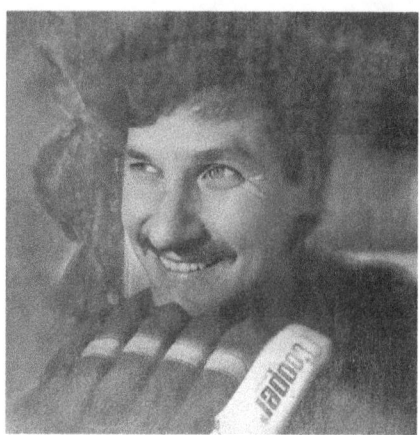

Steve Hertzberg

Steve's wife and high-school sweetheart, Jill Golden, was offered a position as Springfield's first woman attorney ever, so they moved to Oregon in 1975. When Steve heard about the potential for a new rink at the fairgrounds, he jumped at the opportunity and worked to generate community support. Steve would eventually become the first president of the Lane Amateur Hockey Association (LAHA) and a driving force in establishing hockey in Lane County.

Walking toward a meeting at the fairgrounds, he asked someone in the parking lot: "Are you going to the ice rink meeting?"

"No," was the reply, "I am going to the meeting about the horse arena."

They were on their way to the same meeting and entering a conflict that would continue for the next 18 months. Some enthusiastically supported a new ice rink, and others were highly concerned about the future of the horse arena. Steve met Gary Meyer, a figure skater, and UO professor, at the meeting. They quickly bonded and helped form a grass-roots group of skating enthusiasts that eventually lobbied county leaders to convert the horse arena into an ice rink for the recreational enjoyment of the community.

ICE

Ice-skating enthusiasts knew the equestrian community would fight to keep their horse arena. They formed a political action group—which they called "ICE"—to advocate for the construction of an ice arena at the Lane County Fairgrounds.

The Board understood something had to be done, and in addition to financial concerns, overflow horse and livestock waste threatened to impact nearby Amazon Creek. Meyer, the spokesperson for ICE, frequently spoke at events to drum up community support and wrote letters to *The Register-Guard*. Another key organizer, Vance Kirklin, jumped at the possibility of a new rink and joined the ICE committee to pressure the Fair Board. He rallied both figure skaters and hockey players to the cause. Kirklin had competed in ice dance for several years with the Ice Follies and played Junior B hockey in Canada.

Vance, Gary, Steve, and other members of ICE welcomed the addition of a tall bagpiper, Hector Smith, who wowed audiences with his lawyerly charm and hockey stories from his youth. ICE eventually included professional and amateur figure skaters; hockey players from Canada, Minnesota, and New England; broomball enthusiasts; experienced speed skaters; and supporters across Lane County.

Dick Abraham and influential community leaders worked behind the scenes with the county to advocate for the rink. ICE also contacted the equestrian community, suggesting that the ice rink could accommodate horse shows requiring a large seating capacity.

The community speaks

Is the ice rink a good idea?

The *Springfield News* posed the question outside of Bi-Mart on Mohawk, and the responses were generally positive. Attorney Jill Golden said:

Jill Golden (Photo courtesy of Steve Hertzberg)

It's about time! It's 100 percent long overdue! It's outrageous that we've never had a rink in this town. People want to play hockey. There are a lot of people here who used to live on the East Coast and Canada who are hockey players. It's a wonderful sport. We're big supporters of it.

Soon after Jill's interview, a more formal survey, funded by the county, showed strong support for a new ice-skating rink. Of the 400 randomly selected residents:

- over 70 percent had skated before;
- around 60 percent would like to skate on a local rink;
- approximately 70 percent would attend an ice show;
- about 50 percent would attend a hockey game.

The County Commissioners were surprised at the community support and became increasingly interested in the possibility of a new ice rink in town.

In June 1988, the first of three consultant reports indicated that rink operations would generate enough yearly revenue to pay all expenses, contribute to overall administrative costs, and provide a cushion for ongoing maintenance. As a result, the Fair Board authorized preliminary designs and asked County Commissioners to borrow $2 million to convert the current horse arena into a full-service ice stadium and erect a less expensive livestock arena.

On June 23, 1988, the headline on the front page of *The Register-Guard* proclaimed:

REPORT SAYS HOCKEY RINK A GOOD IDEA.

The consultant's report shocked the horse arena's supporters, who quickly became politically engaged. By mid-summer, a new organization — the Friends for a Fair Fairgrounds — had begun to lobby against building a new rink and hired legal representation for a potential injunction. However, the most recent financial report indicated that the horse-arena building had lost more than $46,000 in the previous nine months.

By the time the 1988 summer county fair opened, momentum was with ICE, which had a prominent booth filled with skating enthusiasts. Many skating transplants in the county had yet to hear about the potential of a new ice rink and enthusiastically signed up for the mailing list. The booth and prospect of a novel activity sparked curiosity even for those who had never been to a hockey game or ice show.

One month after the fair, locals gathered in late September for the Eugene Celebration. Again, ICE had an information booth and was signing up volunteers. The weekend's highlight was the Saturday morning Eugene Celebration

Eugene Celebration Parade (Photo courtesy of Eugene SLUG Queens)

parade. With unicycling jugglers, high school marching bands, extravagant floats, veterans in formation, convertible riding beauty queens, anti-nuke activists, vibrant dancers, and comic tricksters throwing candy to the crowd, it was the best introduction to town any newcomer could imagine. At the end of the parade each year, former Oregon congressman Peter DeFazio would follow 20 people dressed as a long slug with his wheelbarrow to scoop up political slime.

Had the 1988 parade marshal understood the rink controversy, he would have placed the ICE group right after one of the many groups with horses, who marched with their wheelbarrows to scoop up the manure.

A WHL team for the 1989-90 season was still on the table, and if construction could begin in January, the ice rink would be ready in time for the county fair and the WHL season. Fair Board member Bill Honsowetz said: "If we don't do it now, we're dead in the water for getting hockey by the time we need to"

The plan was unwelcomed by the Friends for a Fair Fairgrounds. Battle lines were drawn, and polarizing tension between "Horse People" and "Ice People" continued to grow.

There was emotional testimony against the proposed ice rink at the next public hearing. One person said, "I do not want to bury horse-related activities under a sheet of ice," while another stressed, "You have a moral obligation to the horse-riding community."

In January 1989, the ice-arena foes won a victory when the Fair Board voted to delay the construction-bidding process. The Friends for a Fair Fairgrounds questioned the use of hotel-motel tax revenue and threatened court action. "I sense a lack of support," proclaimed Commissioner John Ball, and wanted the project halted immediately.

Newspaper headlines reflected a change in the winds:

THE EQUESTRIANS STRIKE BACK
EQUESTRIANS SAY 'WHOA' TO ICE RINK PLANS

Any hopes for a July completion with a grand opening at the fair and a 1990 Western Hockey League franchise in the fall were dashed. ICE, the countywide group of skating enthusiasts, was crushed.

The local newspaper summed up the ongoing controversy:

It's ice vs. agriculture at fairgrounds

One side dreams of hockey franchise; horse fanciers fear they aren't wanted

The Register-Guard January 22, 1989

The fight dragged on through February, and the Fair Board requested a third consulting report. Property Counselors of Seattle reported that the project would break even financially if they converted the horse arena into an ice rink. The best option would be to attract a WHL team and generate an estimated profit of $50,000 per year.

Horse Trading

To break the standstill, the politicians did what they often did — they agreed to spend more money. In early April, the Lane County Commissioners approved $750,000 for a new horse arena and added $250,000 for a

Dignitaries with hockey sticks and pitch forks at groundbreaking. (Photo Paul Peterson)

warmup area, wash racks, and additional seating. On April 26, the County Commissioners approved the ice rink and awarded John Hyland Construction the contract.

ICE and the skating community were ecstatic. Though the agricultural community had gotten most of what it had requested, horse enthusiasts harbored animosity about the process. Some dignitaries carried smiles and hockey sticks at the groundbreaking ceremony, while others showed up with cowboy hats and pitchforks.

BUILD IT, AND
THEY WILL COME

The *Register-Guard* headlines reflected optimism throughout the fall:

ICE ARENA ON TRACK FOR DECEMBER

NEW ICE ARENA BEGINS TO TAKE SHAPE

NEW FAIRGROUNDS ICE RINK NEARING DEBUT

Lane County hired Kim Brusegaard as the rink's first manager in October. Brusegaard had skated with the Ice Capades and coached figure skating for 12 years. The 30-year-old arrived with significant experience after managing rinks in Walla Walla and Wenatchee, Washington, and was the skating Director for the Ice Capades Chalet in Portland.

The rink's ice would sit atop a concrete-slab rink floor. Beginning in the early summer of 1989, the arena

Kim Brusegaard

construction crew ran two shifts per day, seven days a week. The locker rooms and skate shop were standard construction and completed before the start of the August Lane County Fair. Building an ice rink would require outside expertise, a mountain of materials, and coordinated project management.

Construction materials for the rink included:

- Two miles of copper pipe
- 52,000 feet of steel pipe
- 512 welded joints
- $120,000 of piping, wire mesh, and foam insulation for cooling
- $35,000 for 250 yards of concrete

The concrete pour was the trickiest, and the construction crew hired Harold Lyman from Minnesota to oversee the effort. He had worked on over 100 ice rinks worldwide. It would take 27 trucks and 30 masons working 10-plus-hour days to complete the project at Lane County Ice.

Lyman intently smoked cigarettes as he carefully watched the progress. Once a pour begins, it cannot be halted. On a rainy November day, the crew was running four hours behind. There was a lot to worry about. The supervisor paced up and down the area with Lyman, his project manager from St. Paul, Minnesota. The massive seamless slab could not vary more than one-eighth of an inch over 16,320 square feet. The contractors used a laser measuring device to check the precision of the pour. Tension was high. The concrete would blow everywhere if the pressurized pipes were even slightly damaged. Finally, in the pitch-black early evening, they completed the pour and breathed a sigh of relief.

The final step was to build the first ice surface in Lane County since the closing of the Eugene Ice Arena in 1949. First, refrigeration compressors dropped the concrete floor temperature by three degrees an hour until it reached 10 degrees Fahrenheit. Next, fire hoses equally dispersing cold water would lay down the ice. The crew then applied floor markings, and a used Zamboni rounded the 85-by-192-foot rink to resurface the ice floor.

On Thursday, December 21, 1989, the rink was ready for the people and for the future.

PART II

A NEW ERA

1990

I never realized how much I missed speed skating until they opened this thing. It's so much a part of my life again.

ELMARS BITTE
Eugene Speed Skating Club Coach

You developed lifelong friendships. It was a great way for me to break into the community because hockey is a different, totally different type of situation.

DAN SCHNEIDERHAN
Eugene Blues hockey player

THE GRAND OPENING

I n the first few weeks of LCI operations, public skating attendance and season-pass sales far exceeded expectations. The initial community response was overwhelmingly positive.

One month after the soft opening, county officials were delighted to attend LCI's grand opening on Saturday, January 14, 1990. They assisted with the ribbon-cutting ceremony and enjoyed a piece of the 12-foot-by-6-foot white cake garnished with the rink's blue logo. Commissioner Jerry Rust, a long-time supporter of the rink, was pleased to skate a complete lap without falling before the estimated crowd of over 2,500. The day included hockey games, a Muscular Dystrophy Association celebrity broomball challenge, and a speed skating demonstration. In the afternoon, there was a figure skating exhibition featuring world-class Portland skater Tonya Harding.

A Rising Star

That wasn't Tonya Harding's first visit to Eugene. She had visited the Crest Drive Elementary School in 1987, and *The Register-Guard* headline proclaimed:

OREGON'S ICE PRINCESS
THRILLS YOUNGSTERS

Tonya Harding with young fans (Photo courtesy of Amy Adams-Schauer)

She wowed the students with video clips of her performances at Skate America and spoke to them candidly about her life as a competitive figure skater.

Harding performed at LCI three times in the rink's first year. In addition to the grand opening, Harding skated in the first Summer Fair Ice Show and the inaugural December Holiday Show. The following year, she became the U.S. Figure Skating champion, world silver medalist, and the first American woman to successfully land a triple Axel in competition. People recall her as kind, professional, and generous whenever she visited Eugene. Those attending Harding's performances were fortunate to see such an athletic and talented skater in person.

Years later, Tonya would say:

> Oh my god, Lane County Ice Arena. Oh, I remember that so well. Everybody was so awesome and doing the jump seminars and the skating was truly amazing.

LAHA BEGINS

LAHA Logo (Photo courtesy of Poppie Design)

The hockey association had sprung into action well before the grand opening. Steve Hertzberg and other leaders of the hockey group decided to mimic the name of a similar organization two hours north: The Portland Amateur Hockey Association (PAHA) had been operating since 1961. Seeing no reason to change a good thing, the Lane Amateur Hockey Association (LAHA) was formed as a nonprofit organization in January 1990. LAHA provided governance for all hockey-related activities until 1996, when adult-hockey oversight shifted to the rink. However, youth hockey at the rink continued under the LAHA umbrella.

Bill Poppie of Poppie Design created the first LAHA logo. Bill was another member of the community with deep skating roots. He grew up in Minnesota and played goalie throughout high school and college. When the league began, Bill signed up to be a goalie. Amazingly, eight experienced goalies were living in Lane County; however, the league needed only seven. The team from Vancouver, Washington, had their own. Bill was a good goalie but also an outstanding skater, so he signed up as a forward and would go on to play in the league for over three decades.

Poppie Design stayed involved with the ice rink. They produced a calendar, Women of the Xtreme, as a fundraiser for the local all-women team and created numerous posters, advertisements, and logos to support the rink over the years. Bill is one of the many professionals who donated their skills — lawyers, dentists, accountants, musicians, choreographers, and construction managers. There were doctors, too, who would conveniently pack a suture kit in their hockey bags — just in case.

Tryouts

The term "tryout" creates anxiety as players recall pressure-packed competitions to make their junior or high school team. Eugene had some excellent hockey players, and most can remember the sting of being "cut" from a team. The tryout was necessary for the first league because no one knew how skilled the hockey players were. Self-evaluation tended to either over- or underestimate a player's true abilities, and in a desire to have the teams

NOTES/ANNOUNCEMENTS

NEW HOCKEY LEAGUE — The newly-formed Lane Amateur Hockey Association is looking for players age 18 or older to play starting Jan. 15 at Lane County Ice. Player skill evaluations will be held starting Jan. 2. The cost of $120 per player includes rink rental, officiating and insurance costs. The deadline for registration is Dec. 30. For more information on the league or if you have an interest in sponsorship, refereeing, coaching or forming a youth hockey league, call Roger Wherity at 342-5074, Craig Brusegaard at 342-4057, or write to Lane Amateur Hockey Assocaition, P.O. Box 70570, Eugene, OR 97401.

LAHA Announcement December 1989 (*The Eugene Register-Guard*)

balanced, LAHA required a skate-around before dividing up the players. The tryout became the inaugural draft, an honored tradition that would occur before each season of adult hockey.

Roger Wherity ran tryouts for the roughly 80 hockey players. Roger was a hockey dad active in PAHA and became an Oregon State Hockey Association officer. One of his sons, Chris, would later become the rink's hockey coordinator and Eugene Blues' hockey team member.

The players skated drills –crossovers, stick handling through orange plastic cones, and shooting on the six surprisingly strong goalies who had played at a high level before arriving in Eugene. Many skaters had equipment retrieved from their parent's cellars or optimistically stored high up in their garages. They arrived with cracked leather gloves, torn pants, hole-riddled hockey socks, and flimsy helmets with a useless strap across the top. Tom Goodrie called the equipment "Smithsonian-esque."

It was surprising to see how many talented players crawled out of the woodwork for a chance to compete at the new rink. The top 25 or so players made up two A-league teams. The other A teams were the University of Oregon Ducks and the International Air Academy Jets, who traveled down from Vancouver, Washington, each week for Wednesday night games. The rest of the players—who had come from as far away as Bend, Grants Pass, Coos Bay, Corvallis, and Florence—were split into four B-league teams.

1960-era hockey equipment (Photo courtesy of Bruce Stoddard)

The Draft

The LAHA draft began out of necessity, but it would become the secret ingredient that made the Lane County hockey community special.

If you played adult basketball or summer softball, you were likely on the same team each year. The same would be true in most hockey rinks across the U.S. and Canada. The key to a successful season is finding balance across the teams. Everyone wants to win, but most players would rather play in a close 4-3 loss than a 9-1 blowout.

Lane adult hockey would not have player rivalries; the draft shuffled up the teams every season. By design, players become teammates with any opponent they had run-ins with previously. The captains met a few days before the league's first game to divide the teams equally. The draft became the secret sauce that made LCI adult hockey the envy of many players across the Northwest.

Brian Duggan, who grew up at the rink playing youth hockey and with the Oregon Ducks, summed it up:

> I think the draft for the adult league is maybe the most important part of why the hockey community is so strong. You take what is already a really close-knit community, and then you shuffle up the adult hockey teams two or three times a year. You force people to truly get to know each other. Since I left town, I played hockey in Minnesota, New York, and D.C. and have never seen anything like it. Eugene is a one-rink town where everyone knows everyone, and it has the draft. That's what makes it unique.

EUGENE FIGURE SKATING CLUB (EFSC)

EFSC Logo (Photo courtesy of Eugene Figure Skating Club)

Figure skaters had helped drive the rink's inception and were eager to return to the ice. They quickly organized a program with group lessons and freestyle skate times under the leadership of Skating Director Kelly Bollenbaugh, a proud Canadian and member of a well-known skating family. The interest level was unexpectedly high. There were waitlists for group and individual instruction.

Initially, the rink followed the Ice Skating Institute of America (ISIA) guidelines for skill advancement. Young figure skaters received bright cloth badges for each level of advancement and proudly sewed them on their skate bags and sweaters.

The Skating Schauers

One family in town, the Schauers, embraced LCI like no other. Amy Schauer would become the President of the Eugene Figure Skating Club (EFSC); her husband, Bob, played hockey in the first LAHA league.

The rink's first season passes sold for $30 for the entire year, and Bob bought one for each of his three daughters: Gillian, Lindsay, and Caitlin. The youngest, seven-year-old Lindsay, wrote in her skating scrapbook: "My dad gave me a season pass to Lane County Ice for Christmas, along with a pair of white skates!" It was the wisest $90 investment Bob Schauer would ever make.

All three of their daughters were born in Minnesota, and skating was in their blood. They immediately took to skating and went to the ice rink every day during winter break. Soon they would be getting up at 5:15 a.m. to make the 6:00 figure skating freestyle session.

Standing: Caitlin, Bob, Amy, and Lindsay. Front: Gillian (Photo courtesy of Amy Adams-Schauer)

Amy and Bob are part of skating's unsung heroes. Any parent or extended family member knows the sacrifices made to support a skater, be it a developing figure skater, youth hockey player, or aspiring speed skater. Chauffeur, patient observer, volunteer, fundraiser, and constant supporter are just a few roles of a skater-parent.

Lindsay, Caitlin, and their friends continued to develop and meet ISIA requirements for certification levels. Spins, jumps, pivots, salchows, and other maneuvers were judged for program rhythm, posture, content, and patterns. The tests were tense and followed strict national guidelines. Skaters delighted in their progression, skill development, and medals.

Gillian progressed quickly, and it was no surprise she performed very well in competitions throughout her skating career. Gillian finished first in the Northwest 12-and-under division in Seattle to qualify for nationals. Larger skating clubs from Alaska and Washington were surprised when a skater from tiny Lane County Ice finished at the top. Some skaters had moved from their homes to stay with families close to the development rinks to pursue Olympic dreams. Losing to a girl from the relatively unknown rink in Eugene was crushing. Some were in tears because becoming a Northwest champion meant so much.

The U.S. Figure Skating Nationals were held just outside New York City. The cross-country trip alone would be the thrill of a lifetime for any 12-year-old. Gillian finished 10th nationally in the Juvenile Ladies competition. Simply competing in nationals was a significant achievement; to finish 10th among all the skaters across the country was remarkable.

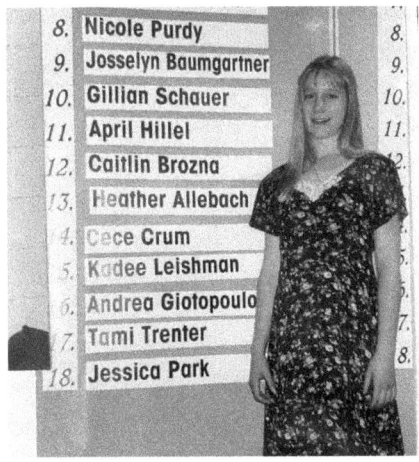

Gillian Schauer (Photo courtesy of Amy Adams-Schauer)

Gliding Forward

Early interest in figure skating had exceeded all expectations, and although finding enough coaching and ice time was a challenge, it was a nice problem to have. The skaters began attending events at other rinks, and after experiencing competitions in Tacoma and Portland, LCI sponsored its own ISIA event in February. Love to Skate became an annual Valentine's Day tradition in 1990 and a popular event for skaters throughout Oregon and Washington over the next 20 years.

At the first locally hosted competition, clubs from Portland and Seattle arrived with bright matching jackets; the local club skated in assorted sweatshirts. Eugene Figure Skating Club designed red, white, and blue jackets and had them produced locally. They held a variety of fundraisers to support the club and sold teddy bears with skates sewn on their feet, entertainment books, holiday wreaths, and sweatshirts with their logo embroidered on the front.

As their membership grew to over 120 skaters, leaders of the EFSC worked to join USFS. They were able to participate in regional competitions and began to host synchronized and freestyle figure skating competitions at LCI.

Some of the mothers of the figure skaters formed an adult drill team. They were more than surprised when someone from Memorial Coliseum called to

Adult Drill Team (Photo courtesy of Cindy Jensen)

ask if they could skate at intermission when the Ice Capades performed in Portland. The women accepted, drove up I-5, put on their red dresses in the locker room, and skated to the crowd's ovation at halftime. Their routines were not quite at Ice Capades' level, but the audience loved them, nonetheless.

LCI was fortunate that several highly successful skaters were living in Lane County when the rink first opened. Competitive figure skater Jan Prasniewski served as a USA Olympic coach. Marilyn Hinson, a Julliard School of Dance graduate, led ice dance choreography, and Kelly Ann Rossbach was a skater with Disney on Ice. In the summer of 1990, the coaching staff and figure skating community organized two events that became annual highlights.

The Lane County Fair's ice show was a spectacular event that showcased the talent of local figure skaters alongside professional stars. The show was a hit among skaters and spectators with its dazzling performances, beautiful choreography, and captivating music. Later in the summer, they hosted a two-week Skate Camp for beginner and intermediate-level skaters. The camp provided skaters with instruction from experienced coaches to help them develop their skills and gain confidence on the ice.

Home of the Brave

Getting up at 5:30 a.m. to dash to the rink for practice is challenging for most young figure skaters. However, one Eugene skater, Emily Monfort, got up at 4:30 a.m. each skating day with no complaints.

Emily was born with Cystic Fibrosis (C.F.)—a brutal, unforgiving disease impacting the lungs and digestive system. When she was born, the life expectancy for a person with C.F. topped out around 12 years. Emily beat those odds and lived for 36 incredible years.

When Emily was seven years old, she went to the LCI with a figure skating friend and later told her parents: "I'm going to do that." Emily was an extraordinary athlete and could do almost anything she put her mind to. She had a strong will and personal strength forged over the years of dealing with her disease. Although Emily's parents, Keith and Peg, understood that skating would take time and commitment, they were supportive from the beginning.

Exercise for children with C.F. is essential, and the cold air at the ice rink helped her breathing. Emily needed an extra hour each morning to take medications (20-to-50 tablets a day); do breathing exercises; receive massage; and use the percussive-therapy machine before she could leave home for the rink.

Emily Monfort (Photo courtesy of Cindy Jensen)

Emily took to figure skating immediately and progressed quickly through the levels. She had grace and balance; her years doing gymnastics at a young age served her well on the ice. Beyond the cool air, the rink was safe, supportive, and fun. Her father, Keith, began taking figure-skating lessons, deciding that participating would be better than sitting around the lobby.

When Olympic gold medalist Scott Hamilton performed in Eugene, he enjoyed spending time with the local figure skaters. As a young child, Hamilton had an illness mistakenly diagnosed as C.F. One year after he began ice skating, his condition disappeared, and many attributed his recovery to the intense physical activity in the cold atmosphere of the rink. When introduced to Emily, Hamilton kneeled by her side as he placed his hand on her shoulder. Scott's kindness and understanding meant a great deal to Emily and her parents. They talked for a long time. Hamilton signed her jacket and looked straight into her eyes.

Scott Hamilton, on bent knee, quietly told Emily Monfort:

> Keep it up, Emily, keep working hard, You have so much to be proud of—good luck with everything.

By fifth grade, Emily was playing club soccer. The growing time commitments for figure skating and her soccer travel team soon became too much; Emily decided that it was time to give up competitive skating.

Many children with C.F. fail to thrive due to physical limitations. This was not the case with Emily. The vigorous exercise of figure skating in the cold rink air contributed to her well-being. She would go on to play soccer at South Eugene HS, climb mountains, become a rafting guide, and graduate from the University of Oregon. She later backpacked across Europe for six weeks—after her first lung transplant. As her father, Keith, would say: "She took big bites out of life."

OREGON DUCKS HOCKEY

Eugene is a college town. Oregon Ducks sports dominate local interest and are a centerpiece of the community's identity. However, most people in Lanc County are completely unaware that the University of Oregon (UO) has a hockey team.

In the fall of 1990, the club sports program enthusiastically approved the application, making it UO's only revenue-generating club sport. At the same time, they also had the highest operational costs. Ticket sales covered some of the costs, but to play hockey for UO that first season, each player on the team paid $1,200 to cover ice time, travel, and related expenses.

A team from UO played in the inaugural season of adult hockey in the four-team A-League. The 15-member team consisted of university students and an architecture professor, Canadian Ron Kellett. The Ducks played in the 1990 winter and summer adult hockey league while they worked to obtain club status.

Scott Brown was the team's coordinator and player-coach. Brown had played high-school hockey in Rhode Island, and when he came to the UO to study architecture, he assumed there would be nowhere to ice skate. However, when Scott heard about the new ice rink, he jumped into action and started recruiting players the old-fashioned way—by posting flyers on bulletin boards and telephone poles. There was so much interest that he coordinated a

Oregon Daily
Emerald

Wednesday, January 24, 1990   Eugene, Oregon   Volume 91, Number 84

Scott Brown (Photo Martin Thiel courtesy of *Oregon Daily Emerald*)

tryout to select the team. The UO Ducks pieced together a schedule with club teams from the University of Washington, University of California, Berkeley, University of Southern California, San Jose State University, and Walla Walla College. The Ducks also played the Eugene Blues in a series of fundraisers.

All they needed was a coach.

Local lawyer and Professor Mike Sobol had been watching the Ducks play in the adult league and took notes. Although he had not played a lot of organized hockey, he was a huge fan. He went to every varsity game at Brown University and while attending law school at Boston University—home to NCAA champions and Olympic heroes.

Sobol left Boston for Eugene and a position on the University of Oregon law school faculty. A few years later, to his complete surprise, two hockey players, Scott Brown, and Darin Varzali, recruited him to coach the team. Mike had secretly dreamed of coaching hockey, so he jumped at the unexpected opportunity.

A matchup against San Jose State was Coach Sobol's first game as coach. Unfortunately, it did not begin well. The Ducks' goalie got a 10-minute misconduct penalty, and Oregon was down 3-0 after one period. However, the Ducks roared back to even the score in the third period. Then, with only six seconds left, they would score to win their first game, 4-3. The team played well for the rest of the year and hosted a postseason tournament where they beat archrival University of Washington, 5-3.

Since club hockey had to be self-funded, business major Darin Varzali — one of two native Oregonians on the team — raised thousands of dollars selling advertisements to local businesses. The team poster featured five players in tuxedos (courtesy of Mr. Tux) standing amid dry ice in their skates. The students loved it.

Ducks in Tux (Photo courtesy of Mike Sobol)

They often practiced at midnight. A few players worked at the rink and could get free ice time if they cleaned and resurfaced the ice. At 2:00 a.m., the hungry college students and their treasured coach went out to find a place for pizza or donuts.

Coach Sobol and the Ducks put many things in place during that first year to establish the foundation for future UO hockey teams. Vance Kirklin, the figure-skating instructor, was their relentless and unforgiving conditioning coach. The team had two assistant coaches, a physician, and two student athletic trainers joining Mike behind the players' bench for each game. Tim Birr, the spokesperson for the local fire department, served as the announcer for each game.

The first Duck hockey team (Photo courtesy of Scott Brown)

The Daisy Ducks, an all-women sports booster group, invited Coach Sobol to speak at the Oregon Club weekly meeting. Sobol followed one of the football coaches, who apologized to the audience for their recent loss to Washington and added that many players were upset and in tears. Mike's first thought was: There is no crying in hockey. He walked to the microphone and informed the crowd about the existence of the Oregon hockey team, then added an impromptu comment to his conclusion: "You know our hockey team played Washington last year and won." The crowd politely clapped. Sobol paused for dramatic effect, then added: "Twice." They hailed him with a standing ovation as he left the stage.

The Register-Guard rarely covered hockey; however, sportswriter Ron Bellamy, taken by this club team's play and love-of-the-game attitude, wrote:

> Once upon a time, all of college sports was like this. No scholarships, no boosters, no NCAA reporting, no worries about bowl games or recruiting. The hockey players, including architecture and business majors, only worry about one graduation rate—their own.

The University of Oregon has had a hockey team every year since 1990 with increasing success. Scott Brown left a lasting contribution to UO when he created—with the support of Coach Sobol and his teammates—the Oregon Ducks hockey program from nothing.

As Scott would say: "It just kind of miraculously happened."

SPEED SKATING

A dult hockey games had begun, figure skaters were working on their routines, and soon Lane County Ice formed its own speed skating club. The leader of the speed skating club was 71-year-old Elmars Bitte, a native of Latvia who had a story to tell. He began skating at five years of age and had placed second in the 1939 European Championships. Unfortunately, World War II interrupted his Olympic dreams.

While skating in the Soviet Union, he met a beautiful woman at the Latvian Embassy in Moscow and spent an evening with her. Unfortunately, this woman had a shadowy relationship with Joseph Stalin. The following morning, while on his way to skating practice, the secret police pulled Elmars off the street into a large black car. He was forced to become a soldier in the Red Army and was sent off to fight in the war. Fortunately, he managed to escape during a bombing raid and made his way to England. Eventually, he came to the U.S., attended medical school, and built a successful career as an anesthesiologist.

Elmars Bitte (Photo courtesy of Ben Strehle)

Elmars was one of the hundreds who lined up to skate on LCI's opening day. He worked with Eugene psychiatrist Bill McConochie to form the Lane Speed Skating Club. John Downen was the club's first president, and Barb Kull, was secretary. They reserved ice time late Sunday afternoons and, at its peak, had about 40 members. Elmars Bitte was thrilled to get back to skating. As the only person with competitive experience, the club named him coach.

He was so excited about the rink, saying: "If they closed it. I think I would move to another city with a rink because it's so much a part of my life again."

Speed skating caught the nation's interest in the 1980 Olympic Games alongside the Miracle on Ice hockey team. Eric Heiden, considered the greatest speed skater of all time, won an unprecedented five individual gold medals. Later that decade, Bonnie Blair won the first of her many Olympic gold medals at the 1988 Winter Games in Calgary, Alberta.

Olympic highlights convinced a small group of young skaters at Lane County Ice to take up speed skating instead of hockey or figure skating. Speed skates are entirely different than other ice skates. Clap skates, translated from the Dutch *klapschaats*, have the blade attached to the boot with a hinge to maintain longer blade contact with the ice so that the legs can move more efficiently. The speed skaters attached thick protective padding to the boards for each practice as they prepared the ice for their biweekly two-hour skate. They placed small cones to form an area equivalent to the short track distance, then moved them every 30 minutes to utilize fresh ice. The skaters, primarily teenagers, had a blast.

One of the newcomers to speed skating was Barb Kull, who first ice skated along the Erie Canal outside her home in Rochester, New York. When the cold winter winds blew, snow floated off the frozen canal, leaving a sheet of ice where one could skate for miles. Barb could gracefully glide down the canal for up to four miles, and at the designated spot, her dad arrived in his snowmobile for the trip home. She wore her family's only skates, a pair of used figure skates. When the ice rink opened in her new hometown, Barb knew that classic figure skating was not for her and tried speed skating. Soon she was getting up early Sunday mornings to join the speed skating club for their workouts. Barb skated with the club for years and went on to write articles for the national speed skating machine. Eventually, Barb and her husband, Stan, a long-time hockey player, moved to the vast beauty of eastern Oregon, occasionally skating on a shallow frozen pond just down the hill from their home.

The speed skating club was able to host many competitions over the years, and at one of the first, a thin nine-year-old inline speed skating champion traveled down from Seattle to race on ice. Apolo Ohno and his father, Yuki, drove down I-5 with hopes of victory in a sanctioned event. Apolo won his event; however, the local club had yet to join the Amateur Speedskating Union (ASU) Foundation, and the race was not officially recorded. Yuki Ohno was unhappy, but Apolo had joined the list of famous Olympians who skated at LCI. Soon after his visit, Lane Speedskating Club became an ASU member and hosted numerous competitions and clinics. Meanwhile, Apolo Ohno went on to become the most decorated American in Winter Olympic history.

The Protégé

To everyone's surprise, a Sheldon High School student would become one of the top speed skaters in the country. Ben Strehle readily admits that he "was really bad at first and could barely stand up on skates." Ben had never ice skated before the rink's opening, but he had strong legs from distance bicycling. Elmars Bitte took Strehle under his wing, and he quickly progressed into a strong, enthusiastic skater.

In Strehle's senior year in high school, he and Bitte flew to Milwaukee, Wisconsin, to visit the new state-of-the-art Pettit National Ice Center. The arena became the Olympic training center with a 400-meter oval for long-track skating. Strehle was hooked: Long-track speed skating would become his event.

Strehle returned to Eugene, but his heart was still skating at the Wisconsin ice center, and when school ended in late spring he decided to cycle the 2,000 miles back to Milwaukee. A friend dropped Strehle off at the other side of the Santiam Pass. With his mother in tears, he embarked on his solo trip across the country.

It took him five weeks to get to Wisconsin, sleeping in farm fields and cemeteries along the way, only to find that the Pettit National Ice Center had been closed for the summer. Undeterred, Strehle stayed, worked odd jobs, and skated almost every day for the next eight years.

THE BLUES

The Eugene Blues filled a void that Lane County did not even know it had: good hockey, quality skaters, enthusiastic crowds, and solid fun on a Saturday night.

When hockey began at Lane County Ice, the rink was astonished to discover how many accomplished hockey players had been lingering in the local shadows for years. Perhaps even more surprising were the 15 outstanding players who formed the first Blues team. LAHA's first president, Roger Wherity, recognized the potential and helped organize the original group. The Blues reflected the geographic makeup of the rink's early hockey days: Mostly guys

The Blues 1990-1991 (Photo courtesy of Chris Wherity). Back Row: Blaise Cassiola, Tom Heer, Tim Washburn, Brad Copeland, Todd Holthe, Tom Bahls, Charlie Boone, Ladia Filip, Curt Geisler, Ron Kellet, Roger Wherity. Front: Earl Erb, Dan Schneiderhan, Tom Goodrie, David Jacobs, Craig Brusegaard, Dick Abraham, Mike Kehoe, Shane Peters, Mike Ronssel, Tom Scutter

from Canada, the Upper Midwest, and New England. One player was from Alaska, and two Europeans were added to the team within a year.

No player had been born in Oregon, although that would change when Coach Wherity's son, Chris, joined the team. The only person from Eugene was the team's manager, Earl Erb. One of the Blues, Tom Bahls, had played high school hockey in Portland, but he listed his hometown as Lexington, Massachusetts.

Dick Abraham was the driving force: With his leadership, things came together in the first two months of the rink's opening. Abraham named the team "The Blues" after Labatt Blue—the world's bestselling Canadian beer—and added a logo to their uniforms honoring his hometown team, the Toronto Maple Leafs. (Beer and hockey are like peanut butter and jelly, although that might give too much credit to the sandwich.) Western Beverage, a Labatt's importer, jumped in as the title sponsor and Papa's Pizza became the team's second major sponsor. With their support, Dick was able to leverage his marketing skills to build the Blues brand quickly—t-shirts, hats, and sweatshirts with the Blues logo were soon available throughout town. The team generally gathered at McMenamins on 19th Street, where a Eugene Blues bumper sticker was prominently displayed above the bar.

Wayne Schantz, who went on to coach the Blues after Roger Wherity, commented: "The whole thing happened rapidly. We're all amazed at how it's taken off with so little promotion."

There were games almost every weekend—Saturday nights at 7:30 and Sunday mornings at 10:30—so the visiting team could get home before work the next day. These were not professional hockey players; they played for the love of the game. Most of the games were at home because so many teams in the Northwest were eager to play at the new rink. After Saturday night games, the visiting and home teams often hit the town together.

The Blues had a solid following of up to 2,000 passionate fans for each game. They sold Labatt Blue beer and Papa's Pizza in the lobby; all the proceeds went to the youth hockey program. Player family members sold tickets, programs, and merchandise in the lobby while loyal fans wrapped themselves in blue blankets as they sat in the cold bleachers.

During every game, the antics of two passionate fans—Heckle and Jeckle—provided comic entertainment by harassing the visitor's bench. Whenever an opposing player received a penalty, they bolted around the arena to taunt the other team from behind the penalty box. Their lively dancing, vibrant costumes, and passionate cheering added color to the already boisterous atmosphere in the arena.

The headline on *The Register-Guard* sports page on April 28, 1990, said it all:

BLUES EARN A NICHE IN EUGENE'S HEART

Dick

Dick Abraham was the Blues founder, leader, and team captain. He was also his high school hockey captain, and his team won the coveted Toronto Metro and Ontario championships in 1972.

Dick had accepted the idea of never playing hockey again when he moved to rink-less Eugene in 1978 as an Emergency Room physician at McKenzie Willamette Hospital. A successful businessman, he stayed involved with the rink long after his playing days ended. His companies, Cascade Medical,

Dick, Allison, Sue, and Nick Abraham (Photo courtesy of Dick Abraham)

Eugene Urgent Care, Nova, and BestMed, sponsored teams each season. The Cascade Medical Blades won LCI's first Oregon senior amateur state championship in 1993.

Handsome Dick was one of Eugene's best hockey players. Always generous with the puck, he would rather have an assist than a goal. Years later, Abraham made it a point to send a scoring pass to Bob Carolan the night before his surgery. Dick picked up the puck after the goal and had a trophy made with the inscription: "Last goal with two kidneys."

The Abrahams were another prominent skating family at LCI. Daughter Allison and son Nick were among the first group of figure skaters at the rink. Nick also played ice hockey and was a member of the first local youth team to win the Northwest championship. Not to be left behind, their mother, Sue, joined the women's drill team and performed with them in Eugene and Portland.

The Manager

Earl Erb was likely the number one hockey fan in the area and jumped at the opportunity to become the Eugene Blues equipment manager. Earl han-

dled the sticks, water bottles, gear, and logistics. As the manager, he became the team's goodwill ambassador, helping with the marketing and interacting with the fans. Earl was the team's devoted and popular manager every season. When the Blues disbanded, he went on to manage the Oregon Ducks hockey team.

The Blues had two primary goals: Provide quality hockey for the public to watch and generate revenue to promote youth hockey in Lane County. They donated all the ticket

Earl Erb (Photo Michael Sheehan)

and merchandise sales to LAHA's emerging youth programs. Their winning record over long-established senior amateur teams throughout the Northwest was impressive. The players were between 25 and 43 years old and were regular members of the community: teachers, welders, salespeople, doctors, students, bakers, and alike. The Blues were essentially the all-star team from the adult league.

Dick Abraham went on to say:

> All of us who played hockey here were surprised at the caliber of play. There are no ex-pros, just solid, all-around hockey players. It's been the missing link for the guys in this area.

The Blues frequently faced off against another talented local team, the Lane County Rangers. In addition to games against the Blues, they played the Duck hockey team and a full schedule each winter against teams from Portland, Washington, and British Columbia. Although the Blues usually took the best local players, the Rangers occasionally beat the Blues—to the delight of the fans rooting for the underdog. The friendly and spirited rivalry between the two teams helped develop the area's burgeoning interest in hockey.

Good Time to Move to Oregon

Danny Schneiderhan moved to Eugene in the late fall of 1989. Little did he know a long-awaited ice rink was about to open in his new home.

Schneiderhan grew up on the Iron Range in Virginia, Minnesota. The Iron Range is home to large-scale iron-ore mining; long, cold winters; small blue-collar towns; and a rich hockey history. His older brother was good friends with Mark Pavelich and John Harrington, who joined fellow Iron Ranger Buzz Schneider on the "Conehead Line" for the 1980 U.S. Olympic Miracle on Ice hockey team. Coach Herb Brooks, who had no idea about the Saturday Night Live Coneheads, had selected three players from an area with a total population of fewer than 40,000.

Schneiderhan was sure his move to Oregon would force him to hang up his skates for good. However, soon after arriving in town, he heard about the new rink opening and went to check it out.

On a cold, not Minnesotan cold, January afternoon, Dan opened the LCI door and smiled. On the ice, Dick Abraham was leading a pickup game with the top players from the adult league. Dan was impressed. "Pretty good hockey," he said to himself. When the Zamboni pulled out to resurface the well-used ice, he lingered in the rink's lobby to talk with a few players who encouraged him to try out for the team. After the next practice, Schneiderhan became a permanent member of the Blues. Years later, Dan commented:

> You know, up there, I grew up watching hockey and playing hockey and playing summer boot hockey. You know, pretty much my life when I was a young kid up there revolved around hockey and fishing and that was about it.
>
> It was totally fun. I mean, it was like playing competitive hockey in high school in front of fans. You know, if you did something, you made a nice pass, a good move or something people would appreciate and cheer.
>
> I enjoyed the games and enjoyed the guys a lot. You developed life-long friendships. I got to know a lot of guys, fishing buddies, biking buddies, winter skiing, and cabin parties on Diamond Lake We'd party, hang out, tell stories, and have a good old time at night. It was pretty special then, and it's pretty special now.

Dan Schneiderhan and Tom Goodrie played on the Blues' first line, with captain Dick Abraham their center. It is a small world; the two wings competed against each other in high school back in Minnesota.

Goodrie, an outgoing and central character in the hockey community, also grew up in a small Minnesota town, Crookston. An excellent athlete, he played college football for two years and went on to the hockey-crazy University of Minnesota Duluth, where he played intramural hockey and broomball.

The Blues at their best (Photo courtesy of Chris Wherity)

The Europeans

Two Europeans, Ladislav (Ladia) Filip and Milan Vatovec, were added to the team within the first year. Both had left their home countries, Czechoslovakia and Yugoslavia, during historic times.

Ladia's father traveled from Czechoslovakia in the summer of 1989 to compete in the World Veterans' Track and Field Championships in Eugene, Oregon. That spring had seen a wave of demonstrations against communist governments in Eastern Europe that would eventually lead to the fall of the Soviet Union.

Eugene was a world away. 10,000 fans attended the opening ceremonies at legendary Hayward Field for a glorious international event that became a highlight in the history of TrackTown USA. Kenny Moore raved about the meet in his Sports Illustrated article, and four-time Olympic discus champion Al Oerter called it "more like the Olympics than the Olympics." Oerter placed first in the M50 division discus competition. In the M60 discus event, Filip Ladislav of Czechoslovakia secured an impressive second place and, remarkably, earned a second silver medal in the shot put. Following his outstanding performance on the world stage, Filip extended his stay in Eugene for nearly a year.

That November, eight days after the fall of the Berlin Wall, the non-violent Velvet Revolution began, and within weeks Communist rule in Czechoslovakia ended. Within two years, the country peacefully separated into two independent countries, the Czech Republic and the Slovak Republic. Suddenly there were new opportunities for young people like Ladia, and he was ready to travel to the West.

In early July 1990, Ladia arrived in Eugene, utilizing the return flight that was available from his father's roundtrip plane ticket. Although his father had returned home, Ladia received support from several of his dad's friends as he settled into his new hometown. The town offered an unexpected bonus for Ladia, who had grown up playing high-level hockey: a brand-new ice rink.

Milan Vatovec traveled to the United States in 1989 from his hometown, Belgrade, the capital city of Yugoslavia at the time. After he left, ethnic tensions grew, culminating in a brutal civil war. In 1991, Milan moved to Corvallis to attend grad school at Oregon State and quickly became a member of the Blues. He often stayed with Dick Abraham for weekend games, who helped him in many ways. During one game, Milan suffered a deep gash from a skate blade, necessitating 17 stitches, while a crucial period remained against their rivals, the Portland Royals. Fortunately, Dick carried his suture to every game, and Milan barely missed a shift. Over the years, Captain Dick stitched up many players while on the bench to keep them in the game.

Oregon was far away from the turmoil in Europe. The Europeans formed an immediate friendship, especially after Ladia discovered that, in his youth, Milan had played hockey in Slovakia. They shared both a Slavic bond and a complementary hockey style. Their play was slightly different, fluidly weaving across the ice into space. Dick could see their synergy and put them on the same line, adding Canadian Ron Kellett to the mix. With their exceptional speed and agility, it was no surprise that they quickly established themselves as two of the top scorers on the team.

In the years following, Ladia Filip and Milan Vatovec were instrumental in the Blues' success while they built their careers in the United States. Milan received his Ph.D. in Wood Science and Structural Engineering from Oregon State and had a successful career as a principal consultant with a renowned international engineering firm.

Meanwhile, Ladia chose to remain in Lane County and focused on his educational pursuits. He earned his teaching certification and eventually assumed the role of physical education instructor at South Eugene High School.

Eddie

When Eddie LeRoy arrived from New York City in 1991, the Blues roster was set, and they showed little interest in the 20-year-old. He quickly joined the Lane Rangers. That season, the Blues and the Rangers frequently played against each other, and Eddie never missed an opportunity to harass the opposing team. The following year, the Blues enthusiastically asked him to join their team. Eddie played with the Blues and the follow-up Ice Hawks until they disbanded in 1999.

Eddie became an assistant coach for the Ducks hockey team in 2006, during their successful run of two PAC-8 championships and several 2nd place finishes. When Scott McCallum left, he became the team's head coach until the birth of his first child, EJ.

Throughout the years, Eddie LeRoy has been a prominent figure in the local hockey community. He continues to leave an indelible and colorful mark on the rink as a star in the adult hockey league, a youth coach, and the Vice President on the LAHA Board of Directors.

A Foundation Set

The Blues' success surprised everyone, including the players. How could a brand-new rink put together such a quality team? The players popped out of the woodwork to establish an incredible hockey foundation for Lane County Ice. They thrived in the Northwest and had a record of 93 wins, 24 losses, and 10 ties over their first three years. Establishing the LAHA adult hockey league was key, but it was the Blues who first showed everyone what hockey could become in Lane County.

BROOMBALL!

By the end of 1990, one more major organization, Lane Amateur Broomball Association, had been established.

It is easy to understand how broomball exists. If you lacked skates, you could still go on the ice and bang around a ball. A wet kitchen broom left overnight to freeze and wrapped in tape would do just fine.

The sport of broomball traces its origins to a game played by the First

Early Broomball in Duluth, Minnesota (Photo courtesy of Broomball.com)

Nations peoples of Canada. The earliest recorded game in the U.S. was in 1910 in Duluth, Minnesota — that state continues to maintain the highest number of broomball players and leagues in the U.S. Broomball is popular throughout the Midwest and is prevalent in Australia, Canada, Europe, and Japan.

Broomball is a lot like hockey, with three forwards, two defensemen, and a goalie guarding an enlarged net — everything but the ice skates. Modern broomball sticks are still called brooms and feature a bright plastic head to slap at the ball.

During the rink's first fall, Eugene Parks and Recreation offered two free sessions for people to try out the game of broomball. Soon after that, Mark Marzullo and Brian Niemeyer established the Lane Amateur Broomball Association (LABA) as a nonprofit LLC by the end of 1990. The LABA league attracted women and men from across Lane County. Word spread through the soccer, basketball, and softball leagues: "Hey, there is a new game you should try." Skating was not required, so less-athletic friends could join the fun. After all, ice is a great equalizer when you are slip-sliding to get the ball. Players in the new league wore sneakers for their first few games, but most would soon purchase special shoes with a sole designed to grip the ice and provide enhanced traction.

The Ice-O-Laters Back: Pete Kensler, Steve Dory, Scott Hubbard, Jeff Kensler. Front: Jeremy Hinds, Mel Carroll, Tom Carroll, Amy Sierzega, and Joanne Harnish (Photo courtesy of Amy Siezega)

Local companies such as Whittier Wood Products, Weyerhaeuser, Comcast Cable, and Russ Fetrow Engineering sponsored teams in the first season and provided long-sleeve shirts featuring their organizational logo on the front. Within a year, the league had expanded to 10 teams and two divisions. Interest in the sport was growing. In addition to their Thursday night games, the rink offered drop-in sessions on Fridays after the Eugene Blues home hockey games.

Single mom Amy Sierzega never wanted to miss a game on her coed team and brought her infant son to the games. He sat comfortably in the penalty box, cradled safely in his car seat, watching his mother play on the ice for the IceOLaters. When Amy checked on her son, he was often asleep, even when joined by an aggressive player serving time. She and teammate Tom Carroll played high-level soccer in Eugene for years but felt that broomball was the most fun — and most competitive — sport they had ever played.

Blues hockey player and broomball aficionado Tom Goodrie talked about the game's popularity in his home state of Minnesota:

> It's basically a drinking game. Oh, come on. Think about it: I mean, it's like curling, but with curling you drink coffee. Broomball, you drink beer — it's perfect!

BUMPS IN THE ROAD

1990 was an incredible first year for Lane County Ice, but there were a few issues along the way.

A Resignation

Just four months after the rink opened, Kim Brusegaard resigned from her manager position, publicly accusing fair management of inappropriate business practices. Brusegaard's allegations included questionable accounting procedures and the backdating of bid requests.

On the rink's opening day, fair manager Steve McCulloch and his wife collected thousands of dollars in cash from customers buying discounted season passes at a table in the arena's foyer. Brusegaard said they placed the money in boxes and did not cross-check with the cash register tapes. She said that, at the very least, it was poor accounting and resigned in protest.

Figure skaters, hockey players, and speed skaters raced to Brusegaard's defense with letters to the editor and public comments. There was universal praise for her work from the rink's user groups and dismay about her resignation. Dr. William McConochie of the speed-speeding club said, "She's very conscientious and wants to do a damn good job for us. I'm concerned about the future of the club."

McCulloch was controversial but strongly advocated building the fairground ice rink. Without his support, the fairgrounds may never have built the ice arena.

The Circus Came to Town

Using the facility for multiple purposes, as initially planned, turned out to be more challenging than anticipated. Big city arenas had the equipment and staffing to convert the flooring in less than four hours; however, Lane County Ice did it the old-fashioned way — by shaving and melting the floor.

The Shrine Club's annual circus was a critical fundraising event for their charity, supporting the transportation and treatment of 300 disabled children. The Shrine Circus had held shows at the fairgrounds for years and planned to perform at the new ice arena. The ice arena was closed for an entire week over the March spring break for two mid-week shows. As rink management saw the cages of tigers, huge poles for the high wire acts, and human cannonball equipment scattered around the rink, they became increasingly concerned about the impact on the arena's floor. Although no cannonballs would crack the floor, the circus was a financial disaster. The contract, tied to attendance, was for $2,000. An average week's revenue was $18,000, and public skating would have significantly increased over spring break.

The circus had a classic Eugene welcome. Animal rights protestors chained themselves to the three-ring circus fence in the livestock arena. The road crew for the circus did not take kindly to the demonstration and immediately put their bolt cutters to work. The activists were kept in the horse stalls until the police arrived.

REFLECTIONS ON
A REMARKABLE YEAR

To celebrate its first anniversary, the figure-skating community put on its first annual holiday show, which included two performances with Tonya Harding. The Eugene Blues also played an exhibition hockey game against the Lane County Rangers—even Santa Claus was in attendance.

To top off LCI's extraordinary first year, the coaches and figure skaters produced a spectacular Holiday Ice Show. The performance became a beloved December tradition with a noble cause. Admission was just one new,

Holiday Ice Show (Photo courtesy of Cindy Jensen)

unwrapped toy for local children. For several years, the Marine Corps Toys for Tots program recognized the LCI community as one of the most generous collection sites, bringing joy to countless children during the holiday season.

LCI income far exceeded expectations. The rink had sold 3,500 season passes, and most of the evening and weekend public-skating sessions were packed. Even the WHL expressed a continued interest. Still, McCullough was slightly disappointed that the rink was not more profitable. Fair leadership expected the ice arena to improve the fairground's finances significantly and cover a larger share of the administrative overhead.

1990 was the ice arena's most successful year, financially. Over the following two decades, mounting economic pressures threatened the stability and sustainability of the rink. The ice-skating community defied skeptical politicians and frustrated equestrians to build the rink and successfully turned their dreams into reality.

Little did they know how hard they would have to fight to keep it.

PART III

MAGIC RIDE
DOWN ICY ROADS

1991-2000

You would go in on a mid-August day and cool off in the ice rink and watch phenomenal skaters like Scott Hamilton, Rosalynn Sumners, and on and on.

BOB SCHAUER,
Figure skater's dad and hockey player

We're excited about being here. We'll be getting players from everywhere ... the East Coast League, the International League, the Central League ...

DAVE DUPAS,
Snowcats Professional Hockey Team coach

ICE SHOWS

The rollercoaster ride of challenges had begun, but there was no hint of concern as the 1991 Lane County Fair opened its gates to enthusiastic crowds for a series of picture-perfect summer days. Despite the excellent weather, the most popular events were inside the ice arena, where Olympic gold medalist Scott Hamilton and Ice Capades members performed spectacularly.

For the rink's first four years (1990–1993), fairgrounds management worked to highlight the entertainment available at LCI throughout the annual fairs. There were hockey tournaments, speed-skating exhibitions, local figure skaters, and broomball games—but the highlight was having some of the best skaters in the world perform for the local audience for free.

Brian Orser, a 1988 Olympic silver medalist and the top-ranked freestyle skater in the world, performed at the rink's first fair. He was joined by, among others, Oregon's world-class skater Tonya Harding, skating legend Richard Dwyer, silver-medalist pair Kitty and Peter Carruthers, and a slapstick group of hockey players skating in costume.

The hockey tournament was an international affair with teams from Colorado, California, Oregon, Washington, and British Columbia. The only Canadian team, the Richmond Flyers, defeated the Eugene Blues in the semifinals and the Portland Royals in the championship.

Scott Hamilton, Rosalynn Sumners, and eleven Ice Capades members performed two shows per day, included in the price of a ticket to the fair.

Hamilton had won the gold in men's singles figure skating at the 1982 Olympics at Sarajevo, and Sumners was the women's silver medalist, with a perfect 6.0 in the compulsory figures. The arena's 3,750 seats were available for free on a first-come, first-served basis.

Fair Program (Photo courtesy of Lane County Fair)

The 1992 "Hot Ice" show again featured Olympic stars, including silver medalists Paul Wylie, Isabelle Brasseur, and Lloyd Eisler. Canadians Brasseur and Eisler had also won silver in the previous year's world pair skating competition. Paul Wylie was especially popular with the local figure skaters. He held several clinics throughout the week, delighting the young skaters and their parents. All the visiting pros were generous with their time, and the opportunity to receive a lesson from one of the Olympians was an unforgettable gift. The ice shows were advertised as "Barn to Skate!" while the hockey tournament's headline was "The Fair's Greatest Hits!"

1993 was the last year Olympians skated at the Lane County Fair. Brian Orser, Kitty Carruthers, and Peter Carruthers returned to the fair for the "Fire & Ice" show, joined by Canadian Olympic silver medalist Elizabeth Manley.

Once again, the world-class shows on Lane County Ice and a hockey tournament were free and included in the fair's admission price. However, the following year, as a growing financial cloud loomed over Lane County, the Ice Shows featuring Olympic stars abruptly ended.

TROUBLE IN RIVER CITY

B y the end of 1990, three factors beyond the rink's control cast a dark
shadow on its future:

- In June, the Spotted Owl was listed as threatened under the Endan-
  gered Species Act leading to a significant loss of revenue for Lane
  County.

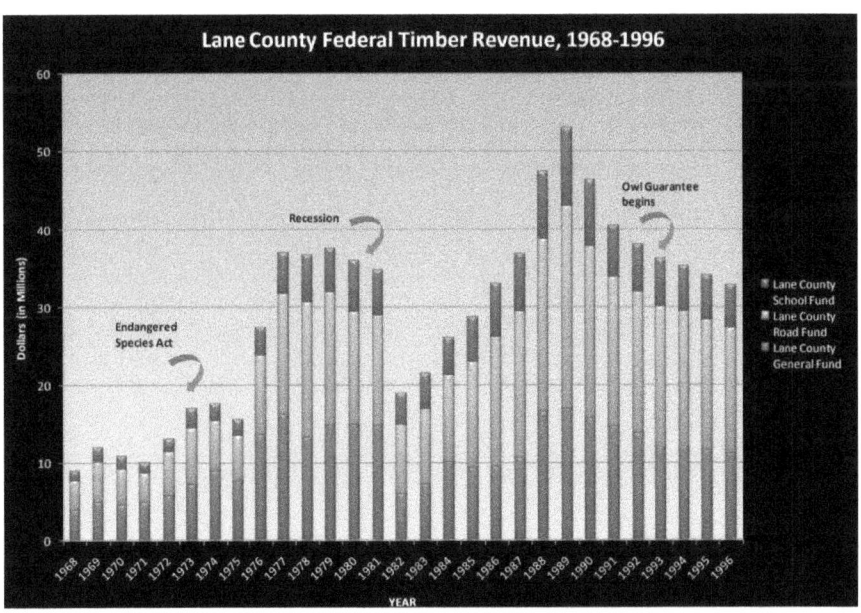

Lane County Timber Revenue (Photo courtesy of Eugene Public Library)

- In November, Oregon voters passed Measure 5, a statewide ballot measure limiting property taxes.

- At year's end, Federal Timber payments to the county's general fund would decrease and continue to drop steadily in subsequent years.

By 1991, the novelty of the new rink had worn off, and public skating attendance significantly declined. LCI experienced a 40% drop in revenue and a budget deficit of $100,000. There were serious discussions about contracting with a private business to operate the arena. However, rink management and the user groups were staunchly against the concept fearing a loss of control.

Throughout the year, *The Register-Guard* had a series of headlines about the rink:

ARENA HAS SLIPPERY OUTLOOK

ICE RINK: DON'T PANIC

INTEREST SLOWS BUT
ARENA NOT ON THIN ICE

The perception was that the rink was losing money, but it was hard to tell for sure. The fair did not include profit for food and beverage in the rink's financial statements, and there was an ongoing controversy about the administrative-overhead allocation. While broomball, figure skating, speed skating, and hockey flourished, public skating attendance decreased significantly from the previous year. Public skates constitute a significant portion of the rink's revenue, and although the $30 season pass was a bargain for skaters, it was a loss for LCI.

The clubs and user groups remained politically active in support of the rink. In 1992, the first in a series of "close the rink" efforts began. A member of the County Commissioners with strong ties to the agricultural community wanted to replace the rink with a livestock arena for auctions and shows. The figure skating club began writing letters and testifying at County Commissioner meetings. A commissioner called club president Amy Schauer and asked her to scale back their efforts and stop writing letters to *The Register-Guard.*

The club did not back down. Children and adults from the skating community showed up en masse at the vote, surprising the County Commissioners who had voted down the proposal. This process foreshadowed the efforts to keep the ice rink open over the next 15 years.

Youth Hockey (Photo Sierra Staley courtesy of The Rink Exchange)

YOUTH HOCKEY

It took a couple of years to build the LAHA Lightning youth hockey program from scratch at LCI. It can be an enriching experience for the players and their parents, but there are significant investments of time and finances to consider. Children of adult hockey players were the first to show up. They began bringing their friends, and within a few years, there were enough players to fill a full slate of teams spanning all the age groups. Some age groups had two levels: a house team and a travel team.

There were a lot of age divisions to fill: Mini Mites, Mites, Squirts, Peewee, Bantam, and Midget.

Many of the better adult hockey players volunteered to coach youth hockey to give back to the community. They included, among others, Mike Kehoe from Massachusetts, Kevin Swingdoff of Minnesota, and Canadian Mike Duggan. Their practices offered more than skating, stickhandling, and shooting development. The players gained important life skills, including teamwork, perseverance, self-confidence, and sportsmanship. The camaraderie of being on a hockey team is hard to find elsewhere, and some skaters became lifelong friends.

Most players began skating at LCI, but one young player had been skating since the age of three on a backyard rink his father had built in Bangor, Maine. Jeff Gibb moved to Corvallis five years later and made the 50-minute drive to the rink multiple times each week to participate in LAHA youth hockey. His dad, Ken, was an experienced hockey player and a welcome additional coach.

The Lightning program continued to grow, and by the end of the 1990s, a team from LCI's won their first Pacific Northwest championship in Tacoma.

Pacific Northwest Champions (Photo courtesy of Dick Abraham)

FAIR MANAGEMENT

The fairgrounds challenged the ice rink for the first two decades to operate efficiently, but the county's complex decision-making structure often got in the way.

The Lane County Commissioners sat atop the leadership pyramid and delegated fairground supervision to the volunteer Fair Board. However, there were ongoing tensions between the groups, and as early as 1990, commissioner Jerry Rust called for the dissolution of the Fair Board.

Steve McCulloch was the fairgrounds manager when the rink first opened. The fairgrounds manager oversaw the fair's operations, including Lane County Ice. Controversy swirled around his business practices, and by August 1992, the fair board was ready for a change. They rejected Steve McCulloch's resignation offer and voted to fire him the week before the annual Lane County Fair. Guy DiTorrice, Star Wood, and Pat Hansen voted to terminate McCullough immediately, while Emerson Hamilton and Sid Voorhees voted to keep him.

Steve McCulloch, the man who spearheaded bringing the ice rink to the fairgrounds, was gone. After McCulloch, Wes Brustad became the fairgrounds manager and increased the pressure on the fair to become financially solvent, with a spotlight on the ice arena.

Tom Bahls followed Kim Brusegaard's resignation only to be forced out due to management conflicts with Wes Brustad two years later. Bahls grew up in Lexington, Massachusetts, home to Revolutionary War battlegrounds and Duck basketball legend Ronnie Lee's high school. Tom became an outstanding hockey player on the ice rinks around Portland and played at Colorado State before arriving in Eugene to work at the newly opened ice rink. He spread his talents around the groups, playing with the Blues, the Ducks, broomball teams, and the adult hockey league.

Bahls embraced the opportunity to manage the ice arena and collaborated with the user groups to create as fair an ice-time schedule as possible. He had several ideas to improve operations at the rink, but upper management resisted. Soon after Wes Brustad became the fairgrounds manager, he terminated Tom and three other rink employees for management and vision conflicts. The ice-skating community was unhappy about another loss of a respected and competent arena manager. *The Register-Guard* headline in July 1993 read:

ICE MANAGER FIRING SOUNDLY CRITICIZED

Skaters and the fired employees spoke at a heated and contentious Fair Board meeting the following week. A terminated supervisor accused Brustad of trying to quell outspoken subordinates, and other speakers criticized Brustad's poor treatment of employees.

The next ice rink manager arrived with great fanfare. Originally from Scotland, John Crosson skated with the Ice Capades in his youth and managed ice rinks for over 25 years. Crosson kept a reasonably low profile but did not appear to commit to Lane County long-term. He and his wife lived in a small RV camper parked at the rink or the nearby KOA campground.

Clint Barnts

Clint Barnts grew up in Springfield and was one of the first employees when Lane County Ice opened his doors. Originally hired as the rink's janitor, Barnts became the key maintenance person and served as the rink's manager for six years. He took on the daily care of the rink equipment, including the compressors, and became an expert at ice resurfacing. Barb Kull of the speed skating club called him "Eis Meister" (German for Ice Master).

Initially, ice resurfacing was done by two well-used Zambonis, a brand synonymous with all ice-resurfacing machines, much like Kleenex or Xerox. Frank Zamboni invented the modern ice resurfacer in 1949 for the ice rink he and his family built in Paramount, California. The first Zamboni at Lane County Ice was old, costly, and frequently in disrepair. When it was time for a change, Clint looked at all brands and decided on the Olympia. Unlike the Zamboni, Olympia runs on a standard V8 engine, and a Chevy dealership was just down the street for service and repairs. Clint Barnts worked to maintain the rink cost-effectively, and his decision to purchase the Olympia saved the ice rink tens of thousands over the years.

Clint was the unsung hero of the rink's early years, working quietly behind the scenes on the compressors and equipment to ensure everyone could enjoy their ice time.

Cindy

Cindy Jensen was thrilled to be skating again when the rink opened and was often the first person on the ice at 6 a.m., loving the sound of blades cutting edges on fresh, clean ice. Cindy began skating in her youth at San Francisco's Legg's Studio, operated by the founders of the premier touring ice show in the country, the Ice Follies. Their home ice was the Winterland Ballroom, which became well known for late-1960s rock shows with the Grateful Dead, Jefferson Airplane, and Quicksilver Messenger Service.

Cindy paired with her brother to perform in amateur shows sponsored by the Ice Follies. They also skated in winter holiday shows for the Christmas shoppers in large showcase store windows and on the roof of the Emporium department store.

Cindy Jensen

While finishing high school and looking forward to college, Cindy hung up her skates, seemingly for good. Instead, she became an educator and moved to Oregon with her husband, a forester, in 1973.

When Lane County Ice opened, she immediately became a figure skating coach. Cindy was an adjunct professor at the University of Oregon and Lane Community College for 20 years. Northwest Christian College followed and offered classes at the rink. Students at the three schools could receive college credits for meeting program requirements in figure skating and hockey skills. Cindy developed a coach apprenticeship program adopted by rinks across the country. After the apprentice completed their training, they received red jackets and became eligible to earn ice time. The participants improved their skating skills and matured into excellent coaches over time. Several apprentices — including Tyee Carr, Kelly Kirklin, Lindsey Moser, Allison Petsch, Casey Sullivan, and Cassandra Vogel — began as young skaters at LCI and progressed through the program into coaching.

Cindy Jensen had a 21-year career as a leader at LCI. She served on the ISI board of directors and held a master rating with the Professional Skaters Association. She would eventually serve as rink manager during LCI's most challenging years.

OPPORTUNITIES

The rink worked to provide opportunities for those with special needs, be they physical, cognitive, or emotional. One of the skaters had Down syndrome. Another needed a wheelchair off the ice, and a young girl with cerebral palsy from the home school program could try skating with her walker.

Farema

Farema Khodabandehloo was born with autism in 1981—well before national awareness of children on the spectrum. In her first ten years, resources were scarce for children like Farema, and little support was available for her family. However, things were about to change. Farema found the ice rink, or maybe the ice rink found Farema.

On a cold December in 1992, Farema and her mother, Lauri, were out for a drive, and while heading east on Thirteenth, Lauri spotted Lane County Ice. *Maybe we could go in to watch*, Lauri thought. Little did they know that the right turn into the rink's parking lot would change their lives and give Farema the best twelve years of her life.

Farema loved to move, as do most autistic children. Once she entered the cool rink lobby, she insisted on skating and soon glided across the ice effortlessly, passing many other skaters. For her first time on ice, Farema's skating was remarkable. Another incredible thing happened that day: for the first time in her life, Farema spoke a clearly formed sentence:

"I like ice!"

Lauri Khodabandehloo beautifully wrote about her journey with Farema in the book *Lonely Girl, Gracious God*. Lauri explains the challenges for her and her family in raising a special-needs daughter. She also writes about the blessings and triumphs of figure skating at the ice rink.

Farema's first day of skating was a pivotal point in her life. She began to talk more; her self-confidence grew; she did better at school and found a new group of friends. The figure skating girls literally embraced Farema with after-performance hugs and sincere encouragement. She suddenly had friends who welcomed her to their team.

Cindy Jensen took Farema under her wing, becoming her coach and mentor, and opening a world of opportunities that had seemed impossible before Farema arrived at the rink. She would compete in the Special Skaters program, win multiple blue ribbons and shiny medals, get her first real job as a skate guard, and reach her goal of skating in front of Scott Hamilton. Lauri's book includes a chapter *Skating for Scott*, wherein she tells the tale from a proud and eternally grateful mother's perspective.

Scott Hamilton, an Olympic gold medalist, has always supported the Special Skaters program and encouraged children with developmental needs to become involved with figure skating. He was Farema's biggest hero. She idolized him after seeing his performances in Portland, the County Fair Ice show, and whenever he skated on TV. Perhaps it was divine intervention when Cindy found a spot for Farema in Hamilton's special training workshop for skaters with disabilities in San Diego.

The workshop was a small part of the annual national conference for top coaches and figure skaters. Farema could briefly skate on half of the ice rink while the Olympic hopefuls practiced on the other end with their coaches. Farema and Cindy worked for months to refine her routine choreographed to music.

When her music began, the coaches and skaters on the other side glanced over their shoulders to watch her skate. Half the rink was not enough that day, and without warning, Farema skated right across the red line to the other

Farema and Scott Hamilton (Photo courtesy of Lauri Khodabandehloo)

side of the rink. The coaches and skaters politely moved to the boards on what had been their half of the ice. Now that she had the entire sheet of ice and everyone's attention, Farema skated her best routine ever. Her flip jump, spins, and lutz jump were flawless, and when the music stopped, Farema gave the crowd a big smile. The ovation was thunderous; those on the ice, amazed at how well she skated, applauded endlessly; those in the stands were standing and cheering. Finally, Farema glided off the ice into the arms of her tearful coach, Cindy, and posed for a photo with Scott Hamilton, who told her what a great job she had done. Farema had achieved her goal in spectacular fashion: she had skated for Scott.

Special Teams

When Max Lester and his Mighty Hawks teammates stepped off the ice with their shoulders held high under sweaty shoulder pads, they looked just a little taller. At that moment, they were not kids with disabilities, special needs, or social challenges — they were hockey players. For Max's dad, Dave, the feeling was "palpable."

Dave Lester played hockey growing up in upstate New York and was thrilled to find that Eugene had an ice rink when he arrived to practice dentistry. Max

Mighty Hawks circa 2001 (Photo courtesy of Dave Lester)

had been diagnosed with Asperger's syndrome and spent time with Dave at the rink, endearing himself to the hockey players. Soon, a handful of other children with special needs were interested in forming a hockey team. Cheryl Halter, a hockey enthusiast who grew up watching the Portland Buckaroos, worked with the rink to establish the Mighty Hawks. Skating instructors provided free lessons for the players to improve their edge work, and experienced hockey players patiently helped them with their stick handling, passing, and shooting.

Dave Lester and Jerry Cunningham, a Canadian-born former Oregon Ducks baseball player, coached. The closest special-needs hockey team was in Colorado, so the team traveled extensively over the years. The Mighty Hawks attended the Special Hockey International Tournament in places like Albany, Toronto, Washington DC, and St. Louis. A few hundred players from across Canada and the U.S. participated each year. The event included opening ceremonies, lavish banquets, and ex-NHL players, making it a memorable and rewarding experience for everyone involved. The tournaments were more than just games: they were opportunities for the players to be recognized and celebrated for their unique abilities.

Over the years, LCI worked to meet the community's unique needs. The tailored programs had a profound impact—far beyond what anyone could have imagined.

NO FREE RIDES

In the lead up to the 1994 fair, the new manager, Wes Brustad, announced:

> The Lane County Fairgrounds is no longer anyone's free ride. Things
> are different in 1994 than in 1964. Timber no longer dominates.
> There are two ways the fairground can survive—allocate tax funds
> to subsidize expenses or users of the fairgrounds can be assessed fees
> commensurate with the amounts needed for operating expenses
> and capital improvements.

Admission prices went up, as did parking fees, and there was a five-fold increase in the cost of unlimited carnival rides. The most significant change was eliminating free ice-skating shows and replacing them with daily concerts requiring an additional ticket. The ice rink was converted into a concert hall—The Concert Stage at the Lane County Ice Arena. The fair organizers had assembled a strong lineup of performers for the inaugural concerts at the ice rink, including Peter, Paul, and Mary; Jefferson Starship; and Tim McGraw. Unfortunately, the following year's fair concert headliners were less impressive: Weird Al Yankovic and Alvin and the Chipmunks.

In subsequent years, concerts tended toward local musicians and tribute bands. Eventually, the fair built an outdoor stage for the headline concerts, and the ice arena was available during the fair for local skating exhibitions and hockey tournaments. However, it was never the same as those exciting first few years.

Wes Brustad's comments went far beyond the fair itself; all users of the fairgrounds would experience increasing fees, including ice time. Still, hockey became more popular, with adult and youth teams competing throughout the year. The figure skating program remained strong, but higher fees and competition for preferred ice time impacted broomball and speed skating.

The two-sheet theory

One solution to the rink's financial pressures might have been a second sheet of ice. Representatives of the rink's user groups formed the Ice Sports Council and sought to convince the Lane County Commissioners that there was a need for a second ice rink adjacent to the current facility. The idea had merit, and VSC Sports Consultants recommended it in their 1993 report. The consultants reported that the rink has an excellent spectator facility and could be the center of attraction at the fairgrounds. Susan Belanger of the Eugene Figure Skating Club wrote a detailed report on the economic impact of a second sheet of ice on the Lane County community. The consultants believed this option was worth pursuing.

Most ice arena experts recommend at least two sheets for an economically viable ice arena. There are obvious advantages, including schedule flexibility and the opportunity to host regional tournaments and competitions. In addition, a second sheet would allow for rotating maintenance so that one sheet remained open in the summer while the other shut down for repairs and recommended care. Consultant Peter MacLeod of Recreation Excellence in British Columbia reports:

> Twinning two rinks provides more revenue per hour, better ice time availability, and increased support for underserved groups. Twinning a rink is a win-win-win.

Unfortunately, Lane County could not take on new capital costs, and the County Commissioners did not even consider the two-sheet concept.

Another option involved a new professional international hockey venture. Rink manager John Crosson was negotiating with the league's founder. It would take some time, but if he could work out a deal, LCI's financial future could be on solid footing.

JOURNEYS
BEYOND THE RINK

Speed skaters, broomball players, figure skaters, and hockey teams all traveled beyond Lane County Ice for tournaments, competitions, and skating events. They arrived back at LCI with memories and stories to tell.

Sun Valley

A group of local figure skaters began going to Sun Valley in 1990 to continue skating while Lane County Ice closed for summer maintenance and repairs. They traveled to the beautiful Idaho valley in winters and summers to participate in camps and competitions throughout the early 1990s. Historic Sun Valley—home to movie stars, Ernest Hemingway's family, and the world's first chairlift—is a great place to visit any time of year. It has one of the country's few year-round outdoor ice rinks and has an additional heavily utilized indoor rink. The Sun Valley Suns adult hockey team has played in the arena since 1975 and, from 2013 to 2016, were senior USA Hockey Champions. Unsurprisingly, Canada's best-selling beer, Labatt Blue, sponsored the Suns.

The skaters, coaches, and parents who were fortunate enough to go on the trips to Idaho experienced amazing times. One year a group of skaters spotted the legendary Arnold Schwarzenegger. Much to their delight, he warmly welcomed them and generously allowed them to sit on his knee while he auto-graphed their sweatshirts. In addition to spotting movie stars, they performed well on the ice and impressively represented their relatively unknown north-west rink. In the 1993 Winter Classic, Lane County skaters placed third out of 35 teams, representing 15 states. The following summer, Casey Sullivan and Molly Hinson were selected to participate in the Sun Valley summer ice show.

Sun Valley's town of Ketchum, a booming mining town in the late 1880s, has a population of just 3,000; the entire county has a year-round population of fewer than 25,000. However, the two rinks at Sun Valley were not enough to meet the skating demand, so the town of Hailey, just twelve miles south, built an indoor ice arena in 2015. The Idaho community's enthusiasm for skating is undeniable, and the skaters from LCI were privileged to be part of it.

Pettit Speedskating Center

Ben Strehle, the Sheldon High School graduate who bicycled across the country, was still in Wisconsin, and a few members of the Lane Speed Skating Club flew to Milwaukee to see him skate on the long track at the Pettit Speedskating Center.

The Pettit is the official U.S. Speedskating training facility. It features a 400-meter oval for long-track speed skating and two international-sized rinks for ice hockey, figure skating, and short-track speed skating. Olympians Bonnie Blair, Dan Jansen, and their teammates regularly practiced at the facility.

The Eugene group happened to be at the rink to watch Blair skate in her last race. She was the first American woman to win five Olympic gold medals. LCI's speed skating club members sat in the stands surrounded by Blair's family and friends as one of the greatest skaters of all time ended her career, easily winning the 500-meter sprint. It was a thrill of a lifetime.

After his friends and former teammates had left town, Ben Strehle's skating continued to improve significantly. He unexpectedly qualified for the 1998 Olympic trials. Ben went on to speed-skate with the America Cup team across the United States and Europe and barely missed making the four-member 2002 Olympic team. At 28, it was time for the Eugenian to retire.

Ben would go on to a successful music career, opening for the likes of Willie Nelson and Robert Plant, while living comfortably with his family on Beacon Hill in Seattle.

Back in Lane County, Arnie Goodman moved up from LA, where he had competed in national tournaments in 1994 and sparked an interest in competitions. The club participated in speed skating events throughout the West Coast, including Portland, the Bay Area, Los Angeles, and British Columbia.

Ben Strehle skating for the America's Cup team.

In addition, the club regularly hosted competitions and clinics at the rink. Diane Holum, an Olympic gold medalist who had set a world record in the 1,500 meters, held a clinic at the rink with participants from across the country. However, with increasing costs for ice and less-than-ideal time slots, the club's membership declined in the late 1990s.

Victoria

The broomball association teams frequently traveled to tournaments and experienced their first international competition when they faced teams from Italy and Canada at an event in California in 1992.

A few years later, the International Federation of Broomball Associations held its semi-annual World Broomball Championships in Victoria, BC. Lane County assembled a coed team, the Castle Nut Knights, to travel north to participate. The event included teams from Japan, Italy, Canada, Australia, and the United States. The competition was intense, and the top men's division allowed body checking; fortunately, this was not the case in the mixed (coed) division.

The Eugene team was excited to venture to one of Victoria's top restaurants, ready to share a meal with their Australian counterparts. Unfortunately, they agreed to split the bill equally in the spirit of international camaraderie—a big mistake. The Australians were heavy drinkers, and when the bill arrived, the Eugene team members were not happy, especially the teetotalers. They also went to dinner with the Japanese team, who had implemented a "turtle strategy" in their games. This tactic entailed the entire team standing in front of their net, inviting the opposing teams to unleash a barrage of shots upon them. The approach, though brave, did not work well against the top-notch competition. Nevertheless, these setbacks failed to sour the tournament experience, as everyone reveled in the experiences with teams from across the globe.

Broomball is a ton of fun, and the players had a blast. However, like the speed skating club, the broomball league experienced a decline in participation over time. The cost and competition for preferred ice time increased throughout the 1990s, jeopardizing both organizations.

Spokane

The LAHA adult hockey was thriving, and in 1995, a team from Eugene first entered the Spokane Old Timers tournament. The trip to Spokane became an honored yearly tradition.

Hector Smith organized the first team for their trip to Spokane. He commandeered the bagpipe band's transportation and loaded players, gear, and "a ton of beer" into the spacious bus. Their trip across eastern Washington was great fun, with lots of drinking and laughs; however, the drive took much longer than expected. Winter had not turned to spring, and the roads were icy, with snowbanks on either side of Interstate 90. At 2 a.m., the bus took the second Spokane exit, slipped on the icy hill, and landed steadily enough to reach the one-star hotel with the cheapest rooms in town.

The distance to Spokane was not the only thing Hector had underestimated. Just south of the Canadian border, the Spokane tournament attracted many strong teams from the surrounding towns and cities. The hockey quality was

Back: Hector Smith, Chuck Selden, Mike Duggan, Bob Weir, Bob the bus driver, John Burns, Sid Magee, Holly Hill. Front: Jody Procter, Jim Herdegen, Terry Smith, David Jensen, Bunk Keggan (Photo courtesy of Terry Smith)

quite high. Eugene's application form exaggerated the team's skill level, placing the team in the highest division. They were dominated in every match and outscored 24-2 in their three games. The team's goalie, Jim Herdegen, was named the tournament's most valuable player. He faced countless shots and made so many saves that his MVP selection was unanimous.

Between games, Jody Procter and Wayne Shantz wandered Auntie's Bookstore marveling at the collection of classic novels, trailed by Bob Weir and Bob Carolyn, who said: "It was like a literature class; they both had read all the books." Many players hung out at the rink, watching other teams play and drinking beer. Hector Smith roamed the stands banging out bagpipe tunes to the delight of the players and the handful of fans watching their games.

Another footnote from the first tournament: the Eugene team played in the last game at the Coliseum. The Spokane Coliseum, home to the Spokane Chiefs of the WHL and the Gonzaga University basketball team, was demolished a day after the Eugene team had left town.

In the following years, Eugene's teams would make every effort to be seeded in the correct division and pull in Lane County "alumni" to join them. Stan Kull regularly traveled from his Eastern Oregon ranch; John Burns came from Portland; and ex-Blues player Chris Wherity lived in Spokane and played with the top Eugene team each year. Every year since that first team arrived, Eugene has sent three or four teams to play at the annual March tournament.

FIGURE SKATING COMPETITIONS

The Eugene Figure Skating Club members frequently participated in regional competitions across the West Coast.

In 1995, Toby Kirklin and Lee Naylor-Watson were regional gold medalists in juvenile ice dancing at the Pacific Northwest Championships and qualified to skate at nationals in Indianapolis. For the first time, the competition would be

Lee Naylor-Watson, Vance Kirklin, and Toby Kirklin (Photo courteously of Cindy Jensen)

called the Junior Olympics and broadcast on national TV. Toby, Lee, and Gillian Schauer were the only skaters from Lane County Ice to compete in nationals.

Local figure skaters regularly participated in USFS regional competitions.

Erika Bulay, originally from the Philippines, relocated to Eugene in 1994. When she stepped inside Lane County Ice (LCI) for the first time, it was a completely new experience as she had never seen or been on ice before. Shortly thereafter, she was leaving home at 5:30 a.m. every weekday to practice skating as she rapidly improved. Erika and Casey Sullivan made the final round at the Junior Nationals in Denver in 2000. *The Register-Guard* reported that their success stunned both the skaters and their parents. However, it came as no surprise to their dedicated coach, Jan Prasniewski.

Casey Sullivan, who began skating at five, knew he wanted to skate professionally after watching Paul Wiley on TV in the 1992 Olympics. He went on to skate for Disney on Ice, performing three shows per day to frequently sold-out shows across the country.

Erika Bulay and Casey Sullivan (Photo courtesy of Cindy Jensen)

Casey and Cassandra Vogel were the only two skaters from LCI to reach gold in freestyle, moves in the field, and ice dance. Cassandra competed in synchronized skating at Miami of Ohio University. After college, she became their skating director, orchestrating the annual ice show, hosting USFS and ISI competitions, and overseeing their prestigious hockey program.

Several Eugene Figure Skating Club skaters transitioned into careers as performers and coaches. One notable individual is Allison Petsch. While at LCI, Allison held various roles, including competitor, coach, figure skating coordinator, and member of the ISI board of directors. In 2010, she and her husband Jay Miller, former coach of the Eugene Generals, moved to Bellingham, Washington. They became co-managers of the Bellingham arena and later moved to Aspen, Colorado, where Allison coaches private and group lessons.

The skaters who performed at regional and national competitions would be the first to credit the invaluable guidance of their coaches. While it's impossible to acknowledge every accomplished skater and coach from the figure

Skating Coaches: Back: Tyee Carr; Middle: Marilyn Hinson, Lindsey Moser, Jan Prasniewski, Kelly Kirklin, Chris Wherity; Front: Cindy Jensen, Allison Petsch, Shannon Young, Vance Kirklin (Photo courtesy of Cindy Jensen)

skating club, it is worthwhile to take a moment to honor the legacies of Don Prebus and Jan Prasniewski, two exceptional coaches who were instrumental in shaping the early days of the rink.

Don Prebus had been a part of ICE, the community action group that campaigned to build the rink at the fairgrounds. He was an accomplished ice dancer known for his willingness to help interested skaters in the discipline and complete their testing requirements. Sadly, Don passed away in 2011. He was 66.

Jan Prasniewski arrived at LCI with an impressive resume, including coaching a pairs team in the 1988 Calgary Olympics. In addition to working with many of the top figure skaters at LCI, skaters traveled from Portland, Medford, and Phoenix to train with him. Unfortunately, in October 2022, Jan's life was tragically cut short after a courageous battle with cancer.

Jan, Don, and all the past skating coaches at LCI have left an indelible impact and invaluable contribution to the rink community.

THE SNOWCATS

E ugene's first professional team, the Eugene Emeralds baseball team, played on warm summer nights in the venerable and historic Civic Stadium, where Satchel Paige had once pitched. Now, the second professional team in Lane County was on its way! In 1995, professional hockey came to Eugene with great fanfare and delight.

Pro hockey was bound to create excitement; one could almost taste the enthusiasm around the arena and skating community. *The Register-Guard* sports page on July 20th proclaimed:

PRO HOCKEY SKATES INTO EUGENE

John Crosson, LCI manager, considered the team's arrival one of the better things to happen in a long time and predicted the new team would double the rink's hockey revenue. The team communications director said the newly created league would have six teams and a 60-game regular season, with 30 slated for LCI.

The Snowcats' owner was Garrett Krause, founder of the newly formed North American League. In 2018, Krause wrote a blog post on *Medium.com*:

> I got ambitious and formed the North American Hockey league
> With minor pro franchises in three countries; Canada, USA, and
> Mexico. We attracted a full slate of players for each team includ-
> ing former NHL players such as Link Gaetz.

A self-described "risk taker," Krause was 28, relatively young to take on such a venture.

Building a new professional league was more of a challenge than he anticipated. Two of the first committed teams, the San Diego Gulls and Bakersfield Oilers, dropped out to play in other leagues. In addition to the Eugene

Snowcats Program (Photo courtesy of Dort Howery)

Snowcats, the league included the Mexico City Toreros, Vancouver Venom, Los Angeles Bandits, and Las Vegas Ice Dice.

Enthusiasm for professional hockey slightly tempered as the calendar moved through August and September. Vancouver could not secure an arena for their home ice and would play all their games away. The schedule included 26 home games and an unknown number of away games.

The Snowcats selected Dave Dupas, a native of Vancouver, B.C. as their coach. He told the local reporters:

> We just arrived in town, and we're excited about being here in Eugene, We really want to work closely with the junior programs, with the kids here. Right now, we are recruiting, and we'll be getting players from everywhere.

Lane County Ice hosted league tryouts in late October, but there did not appear to have enough players for five teams. The Mexico City team drafted tough guys in line with their coach, Mitch Wilson, who was known as an enforcer and frequent fighter during his three years in the NHL.

Dupas selected his team based on speed and skill and assembled a strong team of experienced players in their 20s. Two of their best players were from the Czech Republic. They trained together every day for two weeks before their season opener on November 10th, 1995.

There was concern about the team financing from the beginning, despite their impressive list of local sponsors. Ice Age Entertainment, the corporation that owned the league franchises, was publicly held, and their stock was traded on NASDAQ.

HockeyDB.com, the internet hockey database, reported:

> The North American League was a very short-lived league that has many questions surrounding it. Since the league was a publicly traded company, perhaps the entire league was an investment scam. However, this does not seem entirely likely because some games were actually played.

Season tickets for the Snowcats games sold for $199 and $169. Game-day tickets would sell for $8.50 for reserved and $7.00 with discounts for seniors, students, and youth. They were not simply the Snowcats but the Eugene Snowcats Professional Hockey Club, and every official mention of the team included the term professional. Players generally made a little over $400 per week. In addition, they received additional benefits: free housing, meal vouchers at the Hometown Buffet, free meals at other restaurants, and membership to Gold's Gym.

Their first two games were at home against the Mexico City Toreros, the tough-guy team. They had no Mexican players, only Americans, Canadians, and one Russian. The most well-known player on the Mexican team was undoubtedly defenseman Link Gaetz, whom the Minnesota North Stars selected in the 2nd round in 1988 as an enforcer. Known as "The Missing Link," Gaetz averaged an incredible six penalty minutes per game in his three-year NHL career, as documented on *HockeyDB.com*. His 16-year minor league statistics are remarkably consistent, with a ludicrous average of one minor penalty per period played.

The Snowcats did not back down despite the Missing Link and his team of bruisers. Center Bill McIntosh went head-to-head with Link Gaetz twice, and the Snowcats won their first game 9-6 in front of 2,100 boisterous fans. The play was rough, and each team had 15 penalties, including multiple fighting and game misconducts. Dick Abraham and Mitch Boriskin formed the volunteer medical support team. They quit in disgust after the first game over the ridiculous fighting injuries they had to manage. One player, who had a few teeth knocked out, insisted on returning to the ice for more fighting.

Welcome to professional hockey, Eugene!

Hockey and fighting have had a strange relationship over the years. Many old-timers insist that fighting is just part of the game: "I went to the fights, and a hockey game broke out" is a common mantra. Over time, though, fighting would become less central to the game. There is no fighting allowed in college or U20 international championships. The NHL has adopted more stringent rules to decrease (though not eliminate) fights in their games in an effort to be more family-friendly.

Minor league hockey teams in the mid-1990s considered fighting a badge of honor and a way to advance to higher-level leagues. The Snowcats were no exception.

On November 24 and 25, the Snowcats took on the powerful Vancouver Venom at Lane County Ice. Several ex-NHL players played for Vancouver but that did not intimidate the Snowcats, who ended up winning both games in overtime. Something about the games seemed odd, though, as several spectators spotted players from the Mexico City team skating with Vancouver. Saturday night's game was another rough battle, and Venom's coach was thrown out of the game in the third period for storming the ice toward the referees.

The Snowcats were undefeated and off to a roaring success. Unfortunately, the league would not make it to the New Year, and the North American Hockey League would ultimately become the shortest-lived hockey league ever.

Mexico City

The Cartel did it.

There are various versions of the Snowcats' demise, but those involved agree that the Mexico City trip was the beginning of the end.

The players were excited to fly to Mexico and celebrated with heavy drinking. Many players were hungover when the Mexicana plane touched down in the early evening—not unusual for this group. They were looking forward to crashing at the hotel for the night. Unfortunately, this was not to be.

The bus waiting for the Snowcats at the Mexico City airport had no plans to stop at the hotel. Instead, they were taken across the crowded, dirty city of 12 million directly to the ice rink to play their first game. It would be the only loss of the season for the Snowcats.

There are vastly different recollections of the attendance at the Mexico City games. The players recall a very small crowd, 100-150 attendees. However, Garrett Krause reported that the games were played in front of sold-out crowds of 3,000 at each game.

The Snowcats were bussed back to their hotel and could not leave their rooms due to safety concerns. They returned to the rink, won their second game,

Mexico City poster (Photo courtesy of Bill McIntosh)

and prepared to fly home. However, according to Krause, the Cartel heisted $30,000 in cash from the Mexican arena's back office. He wrote in *Medium.com*:

> The problem was that after the game, "the Cartel" escorted by the Federal Police came in and took 100% or (sic) the GATE Proceeds

(enough said) and it was quickly decided to recall all players out of Mexico and soon after we folded the league.

As soon as the game ended, both hockey teams rushed to the airport to return to the United States. One by one, the Snowcats players left Eugene and flew back to their hometowns soon after returning from Mexico. Some even had to sell their equipment for airfare. By late December 1995, the Snowcats had vanished, disappeared, and evaporated, leaving behind a trail of bounced checks and bad feelings.

The team owed Lane County Ice over $14,000 for ice and rental fees. Co-captain Darren Naylor told *The Register-Guard*:

> I'm really embarrassed for myself and the guys ... Garrett came in with too big a dream. He didn't have the money. Every check he's written in this town bounced.

Krause contacted local officials and media in mid-December, claiming that the ice fees were too high, some of the employees had entered into a conspiracy against him, and he wanted to renegotiate his debts. He said he would send checks to the already-departed players by overnight mail, to which Naylor responded, "That'll happen the same time cows start flying."

On December 16th, *The Register-Guard* reported that Garrett had been arrested in Nevada for writing bad checks, booked into the Clark County Detention Center, and released the next day. There was no communication to or from Krause from that point on.

Only one player, Bill McIntosh, stayed in town. On a clear December

Bill McIntosh

night shortly after his return from Mexico, fate led Bill to witness a horrific stabbing near Sacred Heart Hospital. He valiantly attempted to save the victim's life but was unsuccessful. The District Attorney required Bill to be available for the upcoming trial, and the office eventually hired Bill for a full-time staff position. He remained in Eugene, where he continued to play hockey with the Ice Hawks, a follow-up to the disbanded Eugene Blues. After three tumultuous years in Eugene, Bill asked a friend to drop him off east of Springfield so that he could hitchhike back to his home in Massachusetts. The last Snowcat was gone.

Dort Howery, one of the many unhappy season ticket holders, filed a consumer complaint with the state Financial Fraud division. The state Department of Justice had tried to contact Mr. Krause for over a year and sent Mr. Howery a letter in May 1997 stating that "all letters had been returned and other efforts to contact have been unsuccessful."

Garrett Krause now lives in Florida and has been involved with numerous business ventures, including mineral mining in West Africa and cryptocurrency. Although the Snowcats and the league were short-lived, it was impressive that a 28-year-old could put together such an enterprise. Looking back on the North American Hockey League, he believes that his vision was ahead of the times and further commented in his *Medium.com* blog post:

> The NAL was no scam it was just a bit too early and there was a shortage ice rinks that could fit the crowds we were attracting; we tried, we failed, we learned. It was an interesting venture, I was young and hockey was booming, and we gave it a good try. As far as I know I am the only person to actually host a professional hockey game in Mexico.

Eugene's first and only professional hockey venture ended in sudden failure. The community was left with ill feelings that would linger for years. The Blues disbanded, and although the Ice Hawks replaced them, it was never the same.

POWER SKATING

Soon after the Snowcat debacle, John Crosson resigned from his rink manager position and left town. Mike Gleason, former Eugene City Manager and new fairgrounds manager, restructured the rink management team. Kelly Bollenbaugh, LCI's first skating director, served briefly as the rink manager after John Crosson left town. Mike decided to have a three-person leadership team and promoted Clint Barnts to the manager role, with Cindy Jensen as the skating coordinator and Chris Wherity as the hockey coordinator. The structure worked well. The trio's knowledge, skill, and style complemented each other to form the effective team that Mike had envisioned.

While Cindy, Clint, and Chris worked together, there was a significant change in the adult hockey program. The rink took over the league's administration, and games changed from Wednesday nights to Sundays. Hockey leaders did not initially like the idea and worried about players losing their weekends. Even though Thursday mornings came early, Wednesday was a great night to play. They thought Sundays would be less than ideal and could hurt the league long-term.

Chris Wherity had a plan. Players may have been more skeptical of anyone else, but they trusted Chris to do the right thing. He was easily one of the best hockey players in town after years of playing with both the Blues and the Ducks; he was one of them. Wednesday night ice times limited the adult league to six teams, and opening the league to Sunday games could increase the number of participants. Over the next few years, the adult league grew from 82 to 200 players, and the original two divisions expanded to three—A, B, and C.

The new structure worked. By moving to Sunday, the players no longer had to worry about finances, clean jerseys, referees, and schedules. The rink took over the responsibility, and the only thing that the adult hockey players had to do was show up with their sticks and bags at the right time to play their games. Monday through Thursday were for youth hockey, and weekend evenings were for teams with fans—like the Ducks and Ice Hawks. Sunday became the adult Lane County Hockey League (LCHL) game day from that point forward.

Chris Wherity

Chris Wherity and his dad, Roger, profoundly influenced the rink's hockey program throughout its first decade.

As the 1990 Lane County Fair began, Chris drove down from Portland on a sunny August morning to join his father's team playing in the Inaugural County Fair Ice Hockey Tournament. When he first arrived at the new arena, he was stunned and commented:

> So I walked in, and there was this massive facility with an ice rink, and it blew my mind. I had to pinch myself and say where am I right now because I'm familiar with hockey in Eugene, ever. I was just amazed at how beautiful this rink was.

Chris and his brother, Guy, were outstanding youth players in Portland. Roger Wherity, who fell in love with hockey watching the Portland Buckaroos, was the ultimate hockey dad. Not only did he schlep the boys to and from their numerous hockey events, but Roger also became a volunteer leader in league administration. He served as PAHA president and went on to become an officer in the Oregon State Hockey Association (OSHA).

Chris became a star in high school, and right after graduating, he went to Europe to play in Sweden. He also played junior hockey in the United States

Hockey League and then at Iowa State, where he was a member of the first ACHA Division 1 National Championship team in 1992.

He moved to Eugene in 1992 and played for the Blues while his father was still coaching. After returning to Sweden for the 1993-94 season, he settled in town to attend the University of Oregon. He soon found himself playing for the Ducks and the Blues, working at the rink, and attending school full-time. Eventually, he was named hockey coordinator, collaborating with Clint Barnts and Cindy Jensen to manage the rink operations.

Chris Wherity

Chris's impact on the rink cannot be understated. For example, he worked with the figure skating coaches to develop a power skating class for all skating disciplines. Experienced skaters improved their technique, and new skaters, like Joey Chandler, developed rapidly under Chris' tutelage. In addition to their contributions at LCI, he and Cindy Jensen taught skating classes together at UO and LCC, including a hockey skills class that Chris personally developed.

By 2002, it was time for Chris to move on and pursue further education at the College of St. Scholastica in Duluth, Minnesota. It was a bittersweet departure, leaving behind good friends and an enduring legacy of contributions to the rink's success.

ESPN VISITS

The *Wild World of Sports* began in 1961 and featured sports not typically seen on TV, such as cliff divers in Acapulco, surfers from Australia, rodeos, motorcycle stunts, and bobsled racers. So, it was not a complete surprise when ESPN's version of the program arrived at Lane County Ice to televise the national broomball championship.

The National Broomball Championship at LCI

In the mid-1990s, Lane County became a hot broomball hotbed. Local players went to tournaments in Australia and Canada as members of the US National Team. Lynda Taylor, a recent transplant from Minnesota, served as treasurer on the Executive Board of the United States Broomball Association. One league player, Scott Ankeny, designed an improved stick that was eventually patented. Mark Hunter, a nationally influential referee from Salem, helped bring national tournaments to Eugene.

Spring of 1994 again saw eight teams playing in two divisions. Over the next two years, league play remained strong, and drop-in was more popular than ever, with two sessions going till midnight. An international tournament, Broomball Mania, was twice held at Lane County Ice with teams from Oregon, California, Minnesota, Nevada, Australia, Canada, and Italy.

In 1996, ESPN filmed a special on the national broomball championships at LCI. The televised show featured the final game between two Minnesota powerhouse teams that went to double overtime. It was one of the most intense, competitive, and exciting contests of any sport ever played at the rink.

Whittier Mutant Warriors, "Broomball Mania 8" at Lane County Ice. Back: Bill Pickard, Scott Ankeny, Ben Meigs, Casey Brazil, Craig Edwards, Bob Hobie, Mark Marzullo, Holly Hill. Front: John Wilson, Ron Waggoner, Doug Smith, Pete Melner, Dave Rhodes (Photo courtesy of Mark Marzullo)

After the ESPN broadcast, the once-thriving broomball league play experienced a gradual decline. The eight teams competing every Sunday night dwindled to two. The cost for broomball ice time had significantly increased, and games began at 10:30 p.m., with some starting after midnight. Recruiting new and younger players for late Sunday games proved a formidable challenge.

By 1998, broomball's dwindling numbers ultimately led to the dissolution of league play, marking a sad end to an era of spirited competition and camaraderie. Broomball did not completely vanish from the rink. One might stumble upon a large barrel filled with colorful broomball sticks in a dark corner, ready for play. Church and school groups occasionally find a time slot to rent so their kids can gleefully slide all over the ice in chase of the ball. Sometimes, college fraternities and sororities arrive late Saturday night attempting to play a game. The mid-1990 glory days of Lane County broomball were sadly over.

THE WRITER

J ody Procter, a beloved hockey player, passed away in 1998. He was 54.

Jody was the most famous member of the hockey community—something no one knew until after his death. There were community leaders and respected professionals among the rink's characters, but no one was really famous. One player, Tom Alexander, published a monthly marijuana magazine,

Jody Procter (Photo courtesy of Kit Sibert)

Sinsemilla Tips; another player, Tim Birr, was often on TV as the spokesperson for the county fire department, and Charlie Janz, a big, strong logger and hockey player, had a ski run named after him: Good Time Charlie at Willamette Pass. These were local celebrities, but Jody was famous.

It turns out there is a lot Jody never shared.

Researching Jody's family is like reading a Massachusetts history book. His most infamous ancestor, John Procter, was hung at the Salem Witch Trials in 1692. Notable Revolutionary War relatives include Colonel William Prescott, who told his troops at the Battle of Bunker Hill, "Do not fire until you see the whites of their eyes."

Being born Joseph Osborne Procter IV into a well-to-do Boston Brahmin family came with significant expectations. Jody said going to Harvard was a "family obligation" because men in his family had gone to Harvard practically since the place opened. So, Jody went to Harvard and graduated magna cum laude in 1967.

None of this mattered to the hockey guys. No one asked, "Where did you go to school?" When a teammate asks, "What do you do?" they want to know if you are a forward or a defenseman. No one cared where you went to college or what you did for work. No one cared about the Revolutionary War heroes or the captains of industry in his family. No one cared that videos Jody and his avant-garde collective produced in the 1970s were frequently shown at prestigious museums. The players only cared that you were a hockey player and a good guy. Clearly, Jody was both.

Jody embraced the hockey community, and the hockey community embraced him. He arrived in Eugene in 1991 with his wife, Kit, and 10-year-old daughter, Tara. They had moved from a trailer in Malibu that overlooked the Pacific Ocean. The fact that Eugene had an ice rink was a factor in their decision to move to Oregon.

Like many players, it had been twenty-odd years since Jody played hockey, so he fit right in. He joined the team for the Spokane tournaments, was a member of LCI's inaugural state championship team, participated in league matches on Wednesday nights, and played with the over-35 group on Sundays. Procter hustled, made good passes, and encouraged everyone—be it a

Adult state championship team (Photo courtesy of Bob Carolan)

teammate or an opponent. Regardless, Jody would quietly say, "nice pass" or "nice shot" accompanied by a smile and a gentle tap to their chest. Jody was like that; he was kind.

It ended too quickly, with a cancer diagnosis. As his condition deteriorated, some players visited Jody's home, where a line of colorful Tibetan flags fluttered quietly with the wind. The memorial service was moving; Hector's bagpipes echoed through the crowded Unity Church on Dillard Road. I wore a tie and was surprised that most other hockey players did the same. We sat stoically in the same row, glancing around, unsure of what to do, as the church attendees politely handed boxes of tissues through the largely silent room. Once a box found our row, it somehow gave us permission to cry, and the tears flowed as Bob Carolan slowly arose to read a letter on behalf of the players. (Appendix E)

Jody was a writer. He wrote screenplays, short stories, poetry, and alternative magazine articles. His last book, Toil, was published just after the first anniversary of his death. It is a simple tale of building a house from the ground up. The praise for "Toil" was widespread, with acclaimed author Kurt Vonnegut among its many admirers, and other writers added their praise. Local skaters eagerly shared copies with friends and re-read the book, a testament to the quality of Jody's writing.

Seven days before he died, Jody wrote a commencement speech for the Renaissance School eighth-grade graduation. Here is an excerpt:

> One thing I've learned, and it should be so obvious, is that every day is unique, surprising and precious ... I may have been dealt what looks like a pretty bad hand, but in fact I've come to believe that it is exactly the right hand for me. Why I say this, I'm not exactly sure. But it's a feeling that has come up very strong–a feeling that Everything that happens is the right thing and that it happens in exactly the right way and exactly the right time.

AFTER THE SKATE

There was often a time for fun after games or performances at Lane County Ice.

The Olympians

Following their ice shows at the fair, Olympic skaters and many figure skating club members met for potluck dinners at family homes. It was incredible to see some of the greatest skaters in the world informally walking around in t-shirts and grabbing a hamburger off the grill just like a next-door neighbor. One of the dads, who was also a hockey player, said it was like walking into your backyard, and suddenly, Wayne Gretzky asks if you want a beer.

Some figure skaters were too young to appreciate how amazing it was to share a watermelon with Scott Hamilton, Paul Wylie, or Rosalynn Sumners. However, most skaters knew how special these moments were and kept memories of backyard barbecues with their skating heroes for the rest of their lives.

A few Olympians loved golf and welcomed the escape from practicing and performing on the ice. So, Bob Schauer took them to the Eugene Country Club, which they loved. Golf came easily to these skaters with their athleticism and ability to focus. They were competitive, but it was all about having fun, and Lane County quickly became one of their favorite stops on tour.

High Street

High Street was the go-to place after hockey games. The High Street Café, originally a holdover coffeehouse from the 1970s, was purchased by McMenamins and became the High Street Brewery and Café. McMenamins—a family-owned chain of brewpubs, historic hotels, and theater pubs—also had a pub on Nineteenth Street that some frequented, but most players ended up at High Street for craft beer and respectable pub food. In the winter, a cozy fireplace welcomed the tired skaters; in the summer, backyard picnic tables were available well into the evening under impossibly beautiful bright skies. The servers informally reserved the same two tables every Wednesday night. "Sorry, that table is for the hockey players," they'd say, "They should be here any time now."

Bonds of friendship were forged over pints of Hammerhead or Terminator Stout and Ale-Battered Fish & Chips or a Communication Breakdown burger. Lots of tall tales and laughter filled the evening. Occasionally, someone would share their feelings and describe what a miracle hockey was for them or suggest that the hockey group was better than seeing a psychiatrist.

Sid

The center of Eugene hockey's social universe was undoubtedly the popular and idiosyncratic Sid Magee. From the rink's beginning, he threw himself into the hockey community, organizing the players for epic wilderness adventures and memorial parties at his property on Fox Hollow Road.

Sid came from a different world. He grew up surrounded by the privileged and elite of Greenwich, Connecticut, attending prestigious schools like Country Day, Andover Academy, MIT, and Yale. Sid played freshman hockey at MIT but left college his junior year to vagabond across Europe, Iran, and India. While traveling, he met Oregonian Neil Goldschmidt, who was coaching basketball on an Israeli kibbutz. After their travels together, Sid visited Neil's home in South Eugene, moved back east, and transferred to Yale to study architecture. Goldschmidt went on to become governor of Oregon.

After a divorce, Sid returned to Oregon, towing his Suburban RV and his son, Pickens. Years later, he would reflect on his life and experiences in a 685-page autobiography, an open letter to his son entitled *Pickens*. Sid found renewed happiness and a sense of belonging in Eugene, where he embraced the beauty of the Pacific Northwest with ambitious river trips and snow-camping adventures. He loved that the lush green woods were only a short 15-minute drive from downtown and purchased a 15-acre plot of land in the shadow of Spencer's Butte. Over time Sid built his dream house with a unique architectural design that he chronicled in his first book, *Simple Building*.

In the first season, Sid played for Team Athletic, which was quickly named "Team Pathetic" due to their lowly standing in the league. However, he found great joy in seeing Pickens join the team and play in the final games once he turned 18, even scoring a goal in their last game.

The Fox Hollow parties were legendary. Once they roasted a pig, another party showcased the cooking of Zenon's chef, defenseman Tim Washburn, and at one memorable gathering, they held an exorcism under a July full moon.

Tom Goodrie was in a scoring slump. As one of the area's top players, he was often among the league's scoring leaders. However, he had failed to score in the past four games, and his teammates were concerned about their season. In almost any other setting, it would not have been a big deal — this was, after all, beer league hockey in Oregon. However, Sid, John Walsh, and Tom's other teammates felt they needed something drastic to end his scoring slump.

Fortunately, Paul Reilly's girlfriend came to the party dressed as a shaman. She enthusiastically joined the ritual and delivered a Spanish incantation at an altar of stumps, chicken feet, stones, deer antlers, and candles. Next, John Walsh gave a long and rambling speech in front of the raging backyard fire, calling for Tom's stick to be destroyed. While Tom reluctantly retrieved his stick from the back of his car, Sid grabbed a Sawzall from his garage. The partiers laughed hysterically as they threw pieces of Tom's stick into the fire to rid the demons.

The exorcism worked, and Tom Goodrie scored a hat trick in his next game. Afterward, however, he had mixed feelings about the entire event: "I mean, I lost a stick."

Sid Magee's hockey career ended when he moved to be closer to family in Vermont. Reminiscing about the hockey community and why his parties were so special, he said:

> Well, I think they filled some kind of a need. For whatever reason, that bunch of guys really loved each other, and that came out in the tragic times; it came out every night we went to High Street after skating or whatever, and that was the secret ingredient.

ONE LAST GAME

Less than two weeks before he died, Danny LaPoma, weak from cancer and attached to an oxygen tank, played his last hockey game.

All the seats were taken inside St. Jude Catholic Church twenty minutes before Danny's Celebration of Life ceremony began. A long line of car lights moved slowly through the December evening rain up the long driveway off Willamette Street. Hospital co-workers, distance bike riders, youth soccer parents, hockey players, friends, and relatives wanted to pay their respects and share their sadness over the loss of this person they loved and admired. When there was no place in the church to stand, they gathered outside in the rain. Danny loved the rain. Across the dark parking lot stood a tall man sweetly playing the bagpipes. It was, of course, Hector.

Daniel Robert LaPoma passed away at age 46 on November 28th, 1999. He was a talented nurse, outstanding athlete, adoring husband, and fabulous dad to his two children, Claire and Dario. Dan rode his bike almost every day throughout college, to work, and across Europe with his wife, Daisy. He played soccer and several other sports with great skill and intensity.

Danny began playing hockey in 1993. He was one of the excellent athletes who picked up hockey quickly and became a good player without the benefit of playing in his youth. As his skill grew, Danny played with great passion and sportsmanship. If anyone fell on the ice, Danny would stop skating and go over to help the player up. Teammates would kid him, saying he was "too nice" to play hockey.

Danny in goalie gear (Photo courtesy of Mitch Boriskin)

One night Curtis Roney, a large man who lacked control when skating fast, tore down the ice with the puck. Everyone got out of his way except Danny, who, inexplicably, stood fast. Curtis, not Danny, ended up face-down on the ice. To immortalize the incident, Sid Magee penned *The Wreck of the Old Curtis Roney* (Appendix F). based on Gordon Lightfoot's "The Wreck of the Edmund Fitzgerald."

Danny worked in the McKenzie-Willamette Emergency Room, where his co-workers marveled at his patience, skill, and compassion. Dan treated every patient he encountered with dignity and respect, be they a disheveled homeless person or the mayor of Springfield. More than anything, Daniel LaPoma was a family man. He deeply loved his wife and their two children, and they loved him right back. Danny was many things to many people.

Tragically, like Jody before him, cancer took Danny way too soon. Players visited him as the cancer spread. One late fall day, with the sad players gathered around him, Danny commented wistfully: "I wish I could play hockey one more day." The players looked at each other in silence, thinking the same thing. But, one of the hockey guys that day, goalie Chuck Gottfried, had an idea and blurted without thinking: "Maybe you could play goalie."

The ever-present Bob Carolan, LaPoma's pulmonologist, had his doubts when they met the next day.

"What do you mean you want to play? You can't even walk!"

"Yeah ... but I think I could play goalie," Danny replied.

And so, a plan was hatched. Gottfried brought his thick hockey pads to the rink like he did every Wednesday for the Master's pickup hockey game.

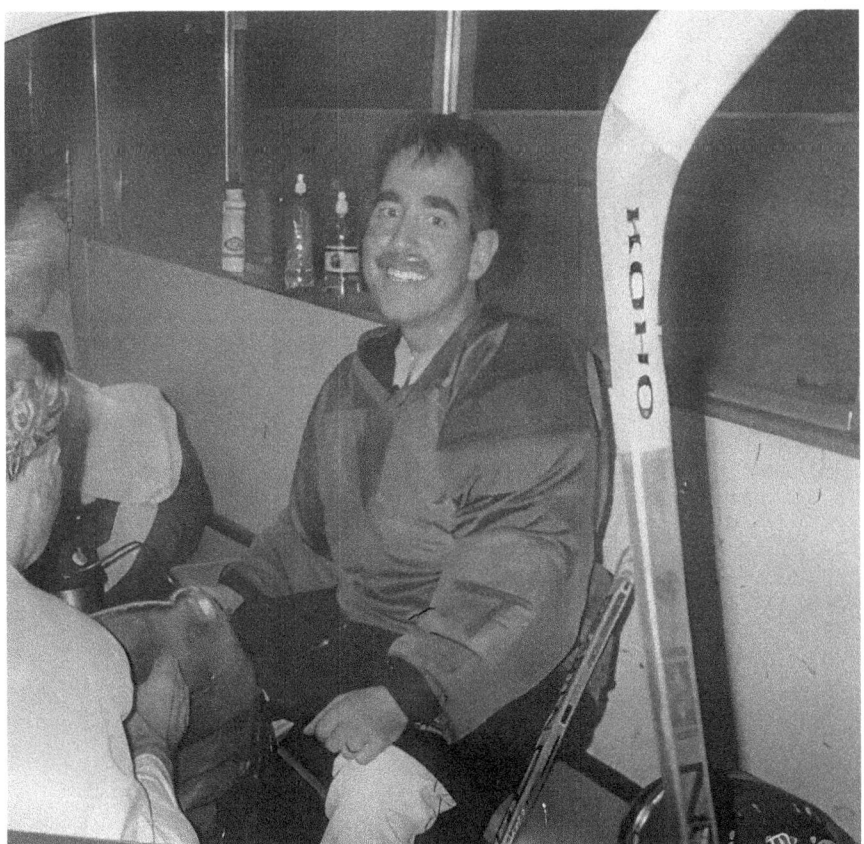

Danny LaPoma after the game (Photo courtesy of Mitch Boriskin)

Meanwhile, his teammates strapped the oxygen tank to the top of the goal, surrounded it with pads, and snaked the 10 feet of tubing through the goal's netting. Chuck attached the oxygen tubing under his goalie pads and helmet. Dan went from the bench to the net and linked the tubes to deliver the needed oxygen.

Carolan had driven Dan to the rink, and their conversation was brief:

"What's the worst thing that could happen?"

"You could die."

They locked eyes, smiled, and gave each other a slight nod.

"Let's do it."

Mitch Boriskin, one of Danny's closest friends, recalled. "He took one step on the ice—one step—and fell right on his back. We all rushed over. I mean, here's this fragile guy. But he was laughing."

Danny stood tall in the goal that evening and made several good saves. Mitch would say that he was ecstatic to be playing one more time. "He was—as we'd say In Yiddish—*Chalishing*, just beaming." After the game, players returned to the locker room. A few were in tears, but Dan kept smiling.

Eleven days later, Danny LaPoma passed away; his story is forever etched in Lane County hockey lore. Karen McCowan of *The Register-Guard* captured the story in her piece:

PLAYER ADORED ON, OFF THE ICE.

When his teammates gathered again on the ice for Wednesday's pickup game, the men all skated to the center of the rink. They formed a circle, took off their helmets, and observed a moment of silence in memory of their friend. Then they pounded their sticks on the ice, skated to their positions, and did exactly what Danny LaPoma would have wanted: they played hockey.

TEN YEARS

What a decade it had been. Rink staff organized a party in the lobby with a giant cake to mark the occasion.

There was a lot to celebrate. Smiles and laughter filled the crowded lobby as skaters recalled the good times over the previous ten years. The journey from the rink's opening had been nothing short of amazing.

The skaters, however, had no idea that the following decade would bring new challenges and threaten the very existence of the rink they loved.

10th Anniversary Cake (Photo courtesy of Cindy Jensen)

PART IV.

THIN ICE

2000-2011

We won three PAC-8 championships, but I think, actually, the neat story is how successful they all became. They didn't just do well as hockey players; they're all doing really cool things. All of them are incredibly successful men.

SCOTT MCCALLUM,
Oregon Ducks hockey coach

If we can't close an ice rink that don't pay for itself, how are we going to make these cuts on women, infants and children?

BILL DWYER,
Lane County Commissioner

THUNDERDOME

Welcome to the Thunderdome!

With the beginning of the new millennium and the rink's second decade, there was a new team in town.

The Eugene Thunder took the ice with the announcer shouting into the microphone and music rocking the arena, welcoming in a new era. Introducing junior hockey was the latest effort to build a solid spectator base for ice hockey. Hockey fans had mixed experiences at the rink with the failure

Eugene Thunder Hockey Club
2001-2002

Eugene Thunder (Photo courtesy of Chris Wherity)

to attract a WHL team and the sudden demise of the Snowcats. The Blues, Oregon Ducks, Rangers, and Ice Hawks filled some of the void, but *The Register-Guard* commented in the fall of 2000:

> Chances of hockey thriving in Eugene have proven to be as slippery as ice.

Junior hockey filled small-town arenas across Canada and the US, and the community had high hopes that the new team would thrive.

The Thunder were a Junior B team in the Northwest Division of the Northern Pacific Junior Hockey League. A Junior A team had been a possibility, but rink management believed that a B team would be a much better fit for LCI. Rink manager Clint Barnes explained that a B team would blend much better with the existing requirements for ice time from the hockey groups, figure skaters, public skaters, and other recreational activities at the rink. A higher division team would require much more ice time and effectively close the rink to other groups on weekend home games. In addition, a few of Eugene's top youth hockey players could compete for spots on a B-level team.

Dean Gorman of Spokane was the principal team owner, and Kelly Hubbard of Williams Lake, British Columbia, was the team's head coach. Hubbard had played three seasons with the Portland Winterhawks after two seasons on a McGill University team which included NHL coach Mike Babcock.

The Thunder recruited players ages 16-to-20 from all over the United States. Junior B teams can have a maximum of two foreign-born players, so they also looked to Canada and occasionally to Europe. They built a solid West Coast recruiting pipeline attracting players from Alaska, California, and Washington. All players paid a $2,500 fee to offset the costs of ice time, travel, and associated expenses. These transplanted teenagers dreamed of turning their talents into NCAA Division-I athletic scholarships, professional careers, or both.

Most players were still in high school and lived with host families while attending Churchill High School. In the ice hockey world, host families are called billet families. Historically, a billet is an official order directing a private home to provide board and lodging for a military member.

A modern-day billet family takes in a young player who has moved away from home to pursue their dream of playing hockey at a high level. The relationship between a billet family and their player-boarder can be incredibly rewarding. The family offers stability in an unfamiliar environment while knowing they are giving back to the community by welcoming the young athlete into their home.

The Thunder played for three seasons and enjoyed significant success, making it to the Junior B nationals in their final year. However, the team's finances became problematic and led to an unexpected ending for another Eugene hockey franchise.

Earlier that season, head coach Kelly Hubbard unexpectedly left the Thunder and was replaced by the team's captain, 20-year-old Kyle Gustafson. Gustafson had a fantastic career as the Portland Winterhawks coach for over 15 years and served one year as an assistant coach in the NHL.

The Thunder's demise was another disappointment for the hockey community. However, a new Junior B team would surface two years later to reignite enthusiasm within the hockey fanbase.

XTREME TEAM

They never had a league of their own, but women have played a significant role in Lane County ice hockey history.

The first season of the adult LAHA league included one woman—37-year-old UO religious studies professor Jane Merdinger. She had played varsity hockey for Brown University in the 1970s and could have easily joined the Ducks in the A league. Despite her contention that she was an "old and battered" athlete, she was one of the top players in the league.

Many women hockey players graced LCI over the years. Law student Roberta Zais was the second woman in the adult league and a welcomed addition to the locker room. The first state championship team from LCI included Karissa Weeks, a grad student at the University of Oregon (UO) who biked to and from every game with her hockey bag strapped on her back, rain or shine. Keri Raygor—who played club ice hockey at the University of North Carolina and won four straight NCAA women's soccer championships with teammate Mia Hamm—decided to join the league after arriving in town to coach the UO soccer team.

The number of women hockey players in Eugene continued to grow, and by the beginning of the new millennium, there were enough to form an all-women team. The Eugene Xtreme traveled the West Coast to participate in tournaments and had a team in the C league. Some members drove from Roseburg, Siletz, and Corvallis to join the team once or twice a week.

Eugene Xtreme 2010 Calendar (Photo Aaron & Annie Jakabosky, courtesy of Poppie Design).

Their games were primarily at out-of-town tournaments, and every year they participated in an all-women event in Vancouver, B.C. Most teams were Canadian, and the Xtreme did not win many games; however, the memories and friendships formed would last a lifetime. The opportunity to play the sport they love with other women is something they always cherished.

After one memorable victory, Alison Kerr, the eldest member of Xtreme, explained: "We beat the Canadians. And I loved having my daughter play goalie and my father in the crowd. It was very special."

For some women on the Xtreme, skating was a family affair. Kellie Hayes' entire family played hockey. Her husband, Chris, played in the C league; her daughter, Chloe, is a goalie; her son, Carter, played on the Mighty Hawks; and the family hosted two out-of-state members of the Eugene Generals. Keeping practice and game schedules for six hockey players was a labor of love—everyone was having too much fun.

Two team members, Julie Pfaff and Jen Bills, got married while at the Vancouver tournament. They eloped between games.

Julie Pfaff was team captain and a strong skater, though she did not begin playing hockey until after age 30. She grew up a few short miles from the Pettit Speedskating Center in Milwaukee, Wisconsin, where she started on a pair of double-runner skates as a young child. Julie picked the game up quickly and became a steady force on defense with both the Xtreme and the ICHL league. Jen Bills also came to the sport later in life. As she turned 40, after years of watching Julie play, Jen decided to lace up her skates and join the team. She jumped right in, playing her first game at a tournament with the Xtreme in Portland. Although off-sides and all the rules took some time to master, Jen was an experienced competitor and came to love the game. She had played rugby for over ten years and was one of the founding members of the UO women's rugby club team.

Jessica Duggan grew up watching her dad and brother play hockey and decided to take up the game herself in high school. After moving on from

Back row: Mandy Hathorn, Chantelle Russell, Sarah Wescott, Ruth Bilder, Amy Buss-Gettys, Kellie Smith Hays, Julie Pfaff. Front row: Tina Tague, Mara Spencer, Jessica Duggan, Jen Bills, Natalie Barrett, Alison Kerr, Goalie: Chase Kennedy (Photo courtesy of Julie Pfaff)

the Xtreme, Jessica played in Portland and organized an all-women's league in Beaverton.

The "Ladies of the Xtreme" forged a lifelong bond as they skated together on sheets of ice across the Northwest throughout the 2000s.

Well-known local radio personality and realtor Mary Reilly described her journey and the impact of skating at the Lane County Ice rink:

> I began ice skating at three, surrounded by my brothers in rural Montana. Sadly, gender roles and age differences kept me from playing hockey with them on our pond. When I moved to Eugene, there was no women's league, only co-ed hockey. I found my comfort zone in the women's locker room, where new players feel safe and encouraged. I've developed quality friendships that extend outside the rink, and I've found it to be a breath of fresh air from the divisiveness that's out there in the rest of the world. At the ice rink, everyone is a skater. All the other labels and expectations fall away; we just leave them at the door. Allowing myself to know the men in Eugene's hockey community has expanded my circle of brothers. I feel like I'm channeling that inner-child/little-sister camaraderie when I skate with the old guys. Being part of the hockey community has provided an incredible sense of belonging, and I sincerely appreciate the encouragement. While we don't all wear the same jersey, we're all on the same team.

Women continue to play a significant role in the hockey community. Some arrive with a rich history of winning state championships or playing D-I hockey, while others with no previous experience join a learn-to-play class and soon move to the C league or beyond.

STRUCTURAL ISSUES

By 2004, Clint Barnts had enough of the challenges at the rink, and Cindy Jensen took over as the manager. Fortunately, Clint stayed as maintenance manager and supported the operation behind the scenes.

Soon after Cindy took the reins, the county dissolved the Fair Board and assumed complete control of the fairgrounds. This action resulted in a total reorganization of staffing and procedures, further challenging the rink's operations.

Former Eugene City Manager, Mike Gleason, served briefly as the fair manager, and the county finance director, Warren Wong, followed. Gleason and Wong generally supported the rink and understood its value to the community.

The new manager, Cindy Jensen, faced another significant challenge when Chris Wherity left his position as hockey coordinator. With no new resources, all hockey responsibilities fell to Cindy The ICHL had grown to 18 teams across three divisions, and the scheduling process was as complex as it was time-consuming. *The Register-Guard* came to interview her on a less-than-ideal day and published a picture of Cindy surrounded by scheduling spreadsheets.

Hoyt

Jon Hoyt came to Cindy's rescue and eventually took over the administration of the adult hockey league.

Jon was one of many skaters who started on the ponds of suburban Boston. After college, he headed west to attend grad school at UC Berkeley. Jon helped to organize local hockey at Iceland rink, where Peggy Fleming, Brian Boitano, and Kristi Yamaguchi regularly practiced. After moving to Eugene, he got to know Cindy as a noon drop-in regular and volunteered to help her out. Eventually, Jon would take over the adult league administration—scheduling, finances, and general organization.

Jon had another claim to local fame when he founded Sugartop, the first hockey club sponsored by a cannabis company, soon after Oregon legalized marijuana. The adult league had plenty of beer sponsorships—Oakshire, Ninkasi, Hop Valley, Claim 52, and even a local hard cider company, Two Towns. Jon's Sugartop Hockey Club received two sets of team jerseys, both home and away, that advertised the dispensary.

While Jon successfully coordinated adult leagues, LAHA managed the growing youth hockey program. Figure skating continued its strong presence at the rink through the 2000s with performances, competitions, and clinics throughout the year. The two pillars of the rink were doing well, but the two other user groups continued to decline. The speed skating club had officially ended in the late 1990s, but early Sunday mornings were reserved for speed skaters; a few enthusiastic earlier risers continued their love of the sport.

Jon Hoyt

A few broomballers also continued after their league disbanded. There was an effort to assemble an LCI-based team for the 2004 World Broomball Championship held in Corner Brook, Newfoundland. However, they could not form a complete team, and their trip to the international tournament was canceled. There was at least a silver lining for Tom Kochevar, who took the money from his refunded plane ticket and purchased ice hockey goalie equipment. Tom would go on to be a regular goalie in the league and evening drop-in games. The trip cancellation effectively ended regular broomball at the rink other than occasional fraternity/sorority gatherings on late weekend nights.

The Frost Heave

Something growing under the ice became an even more significant threat than the finances—the frost heave.

The arena sat on top of wetlands. With the high-water table and the ice compressors running most of the year, a frost heave began to build. Over the years, the pressure had built on the rink's floor and lifted parts of the ice. Due to the shifting permafrost beneath the rink's concrete, the boards around the rink began to bend. The fairgrounds had to replace the boards each year, and the corners of the ice began to creep up.

The situation reached a crisis point in 2008. A company from New York that specialized in such issues drilled holes into the floor and determined that the frost heave's depth was up to 16 feet, estimating that repairs could cost as much as $3 million.

That same year the county board selected Rick Reno as the new fairgrounds' manager. He arrived with impressive experience running large multi-use sporting arenas, including the historic Rupp Arena, home of University of Kentucky basketball. Reno sold the board on his vision to build a profitable $20 million performing arts center. Unfortunately, Lane County Ice was not part of his plan, and Rick Reno quickly added his voice to the growing chorus calling for the rink's closure, which would peak in 2010.

OLD GROWTH

Despite the growing frost heave and its impact on the ice, hockey and figure skating continued successfully—as did public skating and other activities at the rink. The old hockey guys, also known as the Masters, were an important user group and critical supporter of the rink's operations since its inception.

Back Row: Dick Abraham, Mitch Boriskin, Mike Duggan, Bob Carolan, Sid Magee, Barclay Brasted. Front Row: Danny Davidson, Bob Weir, Mike DiBitetto, Stan Kull, Bill Poppie (Photo courtesy of Mitch Boriskin)

With a nod toward the glorious old-growth forests that covered much of the forest in the county, Chuck Seldon named the senior team Lane Old Growth as they prepared for Charles Schulz's Snoopy Tournament. In biology, old-growth forests are considered senescent, a scientific term for growing old with a gradual decline. According to author Karen Joy Fowler, these forests are also regarded as unique and worth preserving, "as close to immortality as any of us will ever come."

The name stuck.

The origins of senior hockey drop-in go back to the first hockey season when the Team Athletic captain scheduled a Sunday night practice for his winless team, dubbed "Team Pathetic." The practice time did not help, and Team Athletic ended up in the league's cellar. Nevertheless, a tradition was born, and every Sunday night, the Masters rented the ice for a pickup game with a select group of the old guys.

Bob Carolan was the first to coordinate the group, and Bunk Keggan—who sadly passed away at 76 in 2020—took over administration. Eventually, Mike Duggan became the organizer, the day was changed to Wednesday, and it became known as Duggan's Skate.

The term "drop-in" is a bit of a misnomer. A skater could not just drop in to play; you had to be on Duggan's carefully guarded list. Being on the sub list was certainly no guarantee of playing time. The Masters' skate begat numerous weekly drop-ins, all carrying a substitute list of hockey players, anxiously awaiting a call or email inviting them to join the skate.

Duggan

In Mike Duggan's Ontario hometown, most elementary schools had an outdoor ice rink, a coal stove-heated changing room, boards for hockey, and an oval of ice outside the wooden panels just for skating. Most of the rinks had lights, so after going home for dinner, you and your friends would return to the rink for another game.

The school rink was one block from Mike's home, and he recalls a childhood of basically playing hockey the entire winter. One rink was not enough.

His cozy Ottawa neighborhood also featured two homemade rinks in large backyards for even more hockey or skating practice. The cold Canadian winters were brutal, but the joy of skating made up for it by a long shot.

Mike's feet would freeze after an hour or two on the ice, and terrible pins and needles ran up his legs when he entered the changing room to warm up. But as soon as his feet thawed and he could wiggle his toes, he roared back onto the ice. Freeze … warm … thaw … return … repeat … and stay at the rink all day. Fabulous!

Mike was a good enough skater to play Ontario high school hockey, but it was time to move on and travel after graduation. He worked across North America and landed in places like Wyoming, Maine, Florida, and New Hampshire. One winter, he was a deckhand on a North Atlantic oil tanker.

Somehow, Mike ended up in Eugene; one might say it was meant to be.

With no hockey, he hungered for something athletic, so he played goalie in city league soccer for seven years. Then Mike found and married the love of his life, Marilyn, who had grown up in Eugene. They settled into a life that included his thriving construction company, two children, and weekly soccer games.

Then the rink opened. Mike did not play in the first season of adult hockey, but quickly jumped in and became LAHA's treasurer in the second year. He recalls coming home after his first hockey game in decades and seeing Marilyn as she came into their living room.

It only took one look — just one look — and Marilyn said: "You're not gonna play soccer anymore, are you?"

The Captain

Coordinator, manager, and beloved leader Bob Carolan makes the arrangements when the Old Growth team travels. Growing up in Norwood, Massachusetts, Bob and his childhood friends played hockey after school on the ponds around his hometown. Memories of skating on brilliantly clear black ice, where the bottom of the shallow pond was visible, still hold a special place in his heart. Although he was a talented skater, Bob did not have the opportunity to play hockey for the Catholic high school he attended.

Bob Carolan

After graduating from Harvard Medical School, Bob interned at the University of California, San Francisco Medical Center, at the height of the 1960s. Like many of his colleagues, Bob was not a supporter of the Vietnam War but found himself drafted into the Army. He spent the following year serving as an officer and physician in Saigon.

Bob and his wife Kathleen went to Kenya in the mid-1970s to teach and work as physicians for both underserved and elite communities. Eventually, their journey led them to Eugene, Oregon. While his professional life kept him busy, Bob often went snow skiing and occasionally found himself playing hockey at an outdoor ice rink just west of Bend. The games brought back joyful memories of his youth, but he assumed his regular hockey-playing days were over.

Suddenly in 1989, the county built an ice rink. When Lane County Ice opened, Bob was a solid B player in the adult league. Remarkably, over 30 plus years, his skills have not declined one bit. Bob's teammates consider themselves incredibly fortunate to have him as a player and friend.

The Wanderer

In Eugene, the name Bob Weir brings to mind the Grateful Dead. However, LCI's Bob Weir is a character in his own right, with compelling stories of world travels and hockey tournaments.

Bob started playing hockey at age three on a pond in Caledon East, Ontario. He was a good player and joined a team in the Industrial League. At 13, he

The Kid (Photo courtesy of Bob Weir)

was their youngest player. They played inside a large barn where the ice stayed hard all winter. There was no need for a compressor. It was that cold.

Weir left home at 15 and traveled across North America, spending much of his time in remote British Columbia. He stayed in places like Cape Scott at the northwesternmost reaches of Vancouver Island and the beaches south of Tofino, where Vietnam War draft dodgers once had built primitive homes beyond the reach of lawmen and roads. After that, Bob backpacked across the globe, exploring countries such as Nepal, Indonesia, Chile, Japan, Germany, and Guatemala.

Bob met his ex-wife on the Oregon Coast, had a daughter, and moved to Corvallis, where they started the New Morning Bakery. He moved to Eugene after they separated and was traveling in Mexico when the rink opened. Upon his return, he immediately checked out the rink and quickly became a prominent fixture in the local hockey community.

Bob Weir's brother, Brian, traveled from Nova Scotia every year to play with the Eugene teams in the Spokane tournament. Reconnecting with the guys over the years became increasingly important, and Brian's trip west was a highlight each March. Players often retell the story about the night Brian had a few beers and tears ran down his cheeks as he began to speak. Sharing is not part of the hockey culture. They needed someone from the other side of the continent to articulate what everyone felt:

You guys don't know how much this means to me—you guys drive seven hours, you stop at that crazy restaurant in the Tri-Cities, you stay at these lousy hotels, and every year you welcome me back. You have no idea how much this means to me and what an honor it is to be a part of this group. It's not about the hockey; it's about the bond. It's about the bond.

Larry the Legend

The Old Growth is more of a brotherhood than a hockey team, and losing a member is devastating. Two players who have passed on have signed jerseys hanging from the rafters above the ice they had played on for many years.

Larry McMullen was such a respected and admired member of the hockey community that he became known as "Larry the Legend."

He played varsity hockey at Rensselaer Polytechnic Institute (RPI) from 1958 to 1961. In Larry's senior year, the team went 16-3-1 and played in the NCAA Frozen Four Semifinals. Originally from Toronto, he was happy to discover LCI when he and his wife moved to Eugene in 1995. He quickly became a team captain and sent out a printed page with instructions to his teammates at the beginning of each season. His use of ALL CAPS, **bold**, and exclamation points revealed his seriousness for the game:

DON'T JUST STAND WHERE YOU ARE AND WAIT!!!!!

If you can't make a VERY clear pass to one of
OUR people, chip it **HARD** up the boards.

Forechecking is the name of the game!
Get on their defense fast!!!

Larry was a talented, competitive defenseman who helped his teammates improve their game. Behind his intense game face was a kind, generous, and compassionate person. He took time to mentor and became a trusted confidant for the teenage children of his hockey-playing pals. There may have been a handful of hockey players at the rink who were more skilled, but there was only one legend–Larry the Legend.

Larry passed away in 2012, and many players proudly skate with stickers on their helmets in his memory.

Helmet Sticker (Photo courtesy of Bill Poppie)

A Creative Spirit

Michael Albert DiBitetto, originally from the Bronx, New York, was a dedicated artist and an outstanding goalie. He had a unique approach to printmaking and produced numerous works of Oregon landscapes exhibited at galleries in Oregon and Art Shows throughout the West Coast. He was recognized as one of four emerging young artists by the Fine Arts Museum of Long Island in 1987.

Mike sold his pieces at Eugene's weekly Saturday Market and the Oregon Country Fair. The annual July fair was the alter-ego of the county fair and a colorful way-back machine to the 1960s. The figure-8 path filled with music, jugglers, parades, and pranksters was confusing, even if you were sober. You could locate Mike and his art by the hockey stick hanging from the open-air loft above his booth.

Hockey players had two stops when they wandered around the Oregon Country Fair. Tom Alexander worked at the Nearly Normal's food booth, famous for blueberry pancakes and vegetarian falefels. The booth was an extension of the Nearly Normal's restaurant in Springfield, which prided itself on slow customer service. The fair version had happier servers, but the wait for food was even longer. Hockey guys would get the nod from Tom and go behind the booth for adult beverages and shade.

Mike's booth was less crowded. If you could find the artist's booth with the hockey stick, you were greeted warmly with a broad smile, a big hug, and

Mike DiBitetto

an invitation to hang out behind his booth. He never lost his New York accent but was not a loud East Coaster. Instead, he was soft-spoken, warm, and unpretentious. Mike was welcomed on the ice for his goaltending and prized off the ice for his charm and humor.

He joined a growing list of skaters who left us at a young age when he passed away in 2016 at 57.

THE GENERALS

After a two-year hiatus, junior hockey returned to LCI when Ken Evans and Lee McCarthy led the effort to establish the Eugene Generals in 2005. The franchise joined the Northern Pacific Hockey League (originally NorPac) when it was a Junior B league. Bobby Freeland was the team's first head coach, and Flint Doungchak became the Generals' general manager.

Ken Evans, the Generals' owner, would play a significant role at the rink from that point forward. His passion for hockey began with his son, Ian, a kid who knew what he wanted. Ken and his family were living in Anchorage, Alaska, and when Ian turned six, he asked to join his friends and try out for ice hockey. Ken and his wife evaluated things logically and determined it would be too much of a time commitment for their busy family. As a consolation, Ian received a $10 wooden hockey stick for Christmas.

Ken Evans

That day he began crushing soda cans into the size of a hockey puck and made his parents move the cars out of the garage into the Alaskan winter. Ian spent all his spare time on rollerblades, knocking those crushed cans into a makeshift net. His enthusiasm for the game was evident, and he'd join a local youth hockey team the following fall.

Slowly Ken became involved with the local hockey community. He took the noontime learn-to-play hockey course at the University of Alaska Anchorage with a few other hockey dads. Before long, Ken was helping to organize Ian's travel team and playing adult hockey.

Ken's father founded the Evans Building Company in Eugene, and when it was time to leave Alaska, Ken joined the family business in Oregon. The fact that Lane County had an ice rink was a significant factor in the decision. Ian had become an outstanding youth hockey player and began playing with the LAHA peewee team. Ken became a team representative to the Board of Directors and eventually served as the LAHA president.

The Generals' success in their first season was a pleasant surprise. The Northern Pacific Hockey League included historically strong teams, including franchises in Seattle and Portland. It was clear that the Generals had put together a strong team when they played in the preseason tournament held in Vancouver, Washington, dominating some of the teams. They would break the record for the most wins by an expansion team finishing the season with an overall record of 38-15. On March 4th, 2006, the Generals won

The Generals celebrating the Western Division Championship in their first season (Photo courtesy of The Eugene Generals)

the Western Division Championship Series, defeating the Tri-City Titans in four games.

Lane County was proud of the Generals, who were successful on and off the ice. The players, in their late teens, excelled at Churchill High School and performed community service throughout the year. A passionate group of up to a thousand fans attended their games. The LAHA Lightning youth hockey teams changed their names to the Junior Generals, sporting the logo on their jerseys, sweatshirt, and souvenir hats.

In addition to the enthusiastic crowds, the Generals had an additional home-ice advantage—the frost heave was taking a toll on the ice and the rink's boards. The local team knew where the ice was raised, and were familiar with the uneven boards lining the rink.

However, as they approached the decade's end, the rink's future threatened the Generals' very existence. Like every skater in Lane County, they worried their beloved ice arena could be shuttered for good.

CALM BEFORE
THE STORM

The "Great Recession" of 2008 and 2009 hit Lane County hard, setting the stage for a decisive showdown regarding the rink's future. Throughout the challenging time, the rink continued hosting well-attended public skates, long practices, lively games, spirited competitions, and exciting demonstrations mixed with rare moments of sorrow.

Curling

Curling is a popular sport worldwide and became a trendy spectator sport when the Olympics officially added the event in 1998. In the optimistic days before the rink opened, there were public discussions about whether curling could be a rink activity. However, curling requires a unique ice surface, somewhat "pebbled" rather than smooth, and could not be played on the ice rink as designed.

Portland Curling Club put on demonstrations at LCI during the 2008 Lane County Fair. Although only a few hopeful fans thought curling could make it at the Eugene rink, many fair attendees participated in the curling demonstration. Anyone could slide a few stones down the ice toward the target and take turns sweeping to influence the direction and speed of the stone.

Curling, a marriage of bowling and shuffleboard on ice, requires skill,

Curling (Photo courtesy of Evergreen Curling Club)

strategy, and teamwork. Each of the four team members slides a 44-pound granite stone down the sheet of ice toward the target circles while two teammates sweep the ice in front of the moving stone to adjust its path and speed. The sweepers use long-handled brooms with synthetic bristles to either speed up, slow down, or slightly change the curl and direction of the stone. Teams work to have their stone closest to the center at the round's end, and after ten "ends," a winner is determined.

Local hockey player, Keith McConnell, tried curling for the first time one afternoon at the fair. He grew up in Ottawa and, like most kids, began ice skating on the town's outdoor rink at a young age. Keith started on a pair of double-bladed skates at age three and continued playing hockey over the decades before ending up in Eugene to play with the over-50 group. Keith welcomed the opportunity to try another ice-based sport and found his curling experience that day as "joyful chaos!" He went on to say:

I, like other amateurs, slid the stones down the ice like weightlifters, with the stones going way past the end lines missing the target circles completely, or like weak, tentative children with the stones coming to a stop halfway to the target. And for the sweeping, it was a good workout and challenge, but to no avail regarding the success of our efforts. We all had immense fun that day, but curlers we were not. Would we want to try it again, maybe, but please, give us our skates and sticks and leave the curling to other rinks.

The curling demonstrations sparked some interest but by 2008 and the looming recession, county leadership was in no mood for additional investments in the rink.

Big Tony

2008 marked the sad passing of one of the most well-liked figures at the rink, Tony Chiapuzio. Tony played goalie in the adult hockey league and helped to coach many youth sports teams throughout Lane County. He was known as "Big Dad."

Tony's family asked that, in lieu of flowers, donations be made to the Tony Chiapuzio Memorial Fund. The fund helped cover league fees for those who could not afford them. Donations continue throughout the years, and many players play hockey only with the fund's financial support. A photo of Tony in his goalie gear hangs in the lobby of the rink. Tony's loss was felt beyond the rink, and for years, the same photo hung above the bar at Highland's Brew Pub, a local sports bar in South Eugene.

PAC-8

The Oregon Ducks hockey team performed well each season since its inception in 1990. However, despite their efforts, the club team did not secure a conference championship until 2005. In the immediate years that followed, the team proved itself a powerful competitor, making it to the PAC-8 finals four times in a row; three games were against archrival USC.

The PAC-8 conference consists of club hockey teams from several universities

Celebration with goalie Wren Arbuthnot (Photo Phil Johnson, courtesy of Jeff Gibb)

in the NCAA's Pac-12 Conference, including Washington, Washington State, Oregon, Stanford, Cal, UCLA, USC, and Utah. Meanwhile, the Arizona State hockey team initially began at the club level but achieved great success in Division I.

The USC Trojans have a rich hockey history that is largely unknown. In the 1930s, they were arguably the top university hockey program in the United States.

At this time, USC had no native Californians on their team. Instead, they attracted talented players from Canada, Minnesota, and Massachusetts with the lure of playing ice hockey in sunny, uncrowded southern California, complete with beaches and co-eds. The Trojans swept the feared Minnesota Golden Gophers in a four-game home-and-home series in 1938 and 1939. Another strong California hockey team, Loyola, recruited mainly talent from Northern Minnesota's Iron Range. The Golden Gophers refused to play Loyola when they traveled to California for the USC games to protest their poaching of Iron Range players. It was tough to blame the players, with the winters and all.

During the early days of the PAC-8, USC was the dominant program, winning eight titles between 1998 and 2010. By 2005, however, USC had a worthy rival— the Oregon Ducks.

Coach Scott McCallum is widely credited for much of Oregon's success.

McCallum took over a team with a 2-22 record; in his first season as head coach, he led the team to a remarkable record of 22-4-2 and, after the incredible turnaround, was named PAC-8 Coach of the Year.

Four local players who had grown up playing youth hockey with the LAHA Lightening were core members of the Duck hockey team during their championship run: Jeff Gibb, Brian Duggan, Tyler McCarty, and Matt Lutsch.

Scott McCallum — Coach of the Year (Photo Phil Johnson, courtesy of Jeff Gibb)

The Oregon Ducks had a historically strong connection with the adult hockey league, and adding these local players only enhanced that relationship. Coach McCallum was supported by fellow Ice Center Hockey League (ICHL) players: Kevin Swingoff, Darren Dunbar, team photographer Phil Johnson, and Michael Spino—the strength and conditioning coach. ICHL players provided sponsorships, dental work, marketing support, construction assistance, injury treatment, graphic design, and suture kits in case a player needed stitches on the spot. It takes a village, and there was a unique partnership across the rink's hockey community. The adults rallied behind the Ducks, offering their support in both visible and behind-the-scenes ways while the team gave back as they could, hosting youth clinics and refereeing games.

The Ducks of 2005 entered the PAC-8 tournament as a three-seed. They met the hosting team, Cal Berkley, and their deep bench wore down the Bears as the Ducks reeled off four goals to close the game with a 7-3 win. The victory set the stage for a final game with the Washington Huskies. The Ducks would hold onto a 3-2 lead through a scoreless third period to win the PAC-8 championship for the first time.

McCallum was named PAC-8 coach of the year and, after the win, asserted: "I think before this, we were sort of overlooked, and no one paid attention to us,"

His captain, Jeff Gibb, came from a well-known hockey family. The NHL's Detroit Red Wings drafted Jeff's father, Ken, after being the University of North Dakota hockey team captain. Jeff's uncle, Dave Gibb, is linked to an epic youth hockey milestone: He was on the ice when seven-year-old Wayne Gretzky scored his first goal. Gretzky would become the greatest hockey player of all time and graciously autographed a photo for Dave with the inscription: *To David: The guy who got me started!*

The Ducks would make the PAC-8 finals the following four years and renew their heated rivalry with USC in three straight championship games. In 2006 LCI hosted the PAC-8 tournament, and finals went beyond overtime into a shootout, which USC prevailed to the disappointment of the enthusiastic home crowd. The championship game went into overtime again the following year, and USC scored in sudden death to capture the crown once again.

Bad blood had been building for years between USC and Oregon. The

Trojans are not a particularly dirty team, but they were cocky and easy to dislike. The 2007 PAC-8 tournament was held in Los Angeles, and after their crushing defeat, the Ducks were met by the Trojan student band playing their fight song as they dejectedly walked from the ice rink to the team bus.

Opposing fans often refer to USC as "The University of Spoiled Children." John McPhee took it further in a *PDX Happenings* piece, gleefully describing the Duck's victory in 2008:

> USC is comprised of a bunch of whining, sniveling brats. They aren't well-liked throughout the league, as they get everything handed to them on a silver platter. On Feb 15th, it appeared that their butlers took the day off, or their platters had gone missing because the Ducks owned USC. The Ducks won 5-1, leaving little doubt who the superior team was.

The 2008 and 2009 teams were particularly strong and had beaten Washington State 16-2 in the 2008 semifinals. The following year the Ducks beat Washington for their second consecutive championship. It was a fitting end to the careers of the Eugene-based Ducks Gibb, Duggan, McCarty, and Lutsch. McCallum was again named Coach of the Year.

The teams worked hard but had a lot of fun along the way. The road trips

2008 Champs Oregon 5 USC 1 (Photo Phil Johnson, courtesy of Jeff Gibb)

were a bonding experience, and the team was able to go out together on the town Saturday nights after their away games. Roaming around Los Angeles was a highlight. Someone knew someone who knew someone, and a few players even got into the Playboy Mansion one evening. As with most teams, there are plenty of stories—some for sharing, others not. One humorous tale from the team's travel ended up on national media and spawned a Facebook group: "Moon over Mormon County." In the middle of a rough game, with five players crowded into the penalty box, the USC goalie dropped his pants and mooned the crowd. Unfortunately, the game was in Utah, a state without a sense of humor for such antics. The police escorted the player off the ice and charged him with misdemeanor lewdness.

The name of the USC backup goalie? Matt Buttweiler.

In 2010 Coach Scott McCallum, a specialist at the Eugene School District teaching blind children left town and became a national leader in his field. Eddie LeRoy became head coach briefly, and another adult hockey player, Rich Salahor, coached the Ducks for five successful seasons. Rich grew up playing hockey in Calgary, Alberta, where he became a strong and admired player. After living and playing hockey on Vancouver Island, Rich went on to make a significant contribution to Oregon hockey's history. He was one more example of the adult hockey community's support of the Ducks.

Even with their success, the high-flying Ducks of 2010 had an uncertain future. Their beloved rink, which had provided a recruiting advantage for all these years, faced potential closure. That same year USC beat Washington for the PAC-8 title. However, it would end an era, and USC has not won another championship since, while the Oregon Ducks hockey team went on to win three titles over the ensuing 12 years.

ON THE EDGE

Would they close the rink? The County Commissioners appeared to lack any other politically viable options.

The rink's slow death march had been quietly building since 2000 as the county's finances got tighter and the cost to maintain the ice arena increased. Most skaters had little idea that the ice arena had a target on its back until the situation reached a fever pitch when the great recession hit Lane County in 2008. The coastal newspaper, *Bandon Western World*, reported: "Five counties in heavily forested western Oregon have lost a third to two-thirds of their general funds."

The outlook for LCI—with a known frost-heave problem and perceived annual deficits—was grim. Significant cuts to the county budget were coming.

In 2009, two local newspapers featured stories about the rink's likely demise. *The Register-Guard* said they might find more value in a multi-use arena under this headline:

EUGENE ICE RINK ON THE BRINK

Even the free *Eugene Weekly* chimed in, asking if anyone had $3 million to spare with the headline:

ICE RINK TO GO EXTINCT?

Give a Puck, Save the Rink

With the rink's future at the center of ongoing discussions within the county, several members of the rink user groups sprang into action. They quickly formed a 501(c)(3) nonprofit to represent rink users and gather contributions. The Ice Sports Foundation of Lane County (ISF) had a memorable slogan: "Give a Puck, Save the Rink." Community members poured their hearts, time, and energy into the fight.

Why so much passion about a few inches of frozen water atop a concrete slab, surrounded by unattractive bleacher seats, inside a nondescript off-white building at the southwest corner of a sprawling parking lot?

Well, this building was home to joyful public skates, great broomball games, enduring camaraderie, fantastic holiday ice shows, youth hockey tournaments, lots of laughs, Olympic figure skaters, memorable victories, real tears, speed skating clinics, exercise euphoria, crushing disappointments, parental pride, festive birthday parties, skill development, big hugs, competitions won, a vibrant adult hockey program, and all great fun.

Why? You need ice to skate, so unless your town's temperature stays below zero degrees Celsius for a few months, you need an indoor rink. For most other sports, you do not need much more than a ball and a relatively flat piece of land. However, hockey, figure skating, and speed skating require an arena with a maintained ice surface. Once Lane County Ice was built, many people could not imagine life without it.

The ISF committee included talented professionals: bankers, marketers, accountants, lawyers, computer technicians, communication experts, grant writers, and others with valuable skills. They studied rink financial statements, looked for business partners, wrote letters, built databases, recruited donors, marched in parades, managed phone trees, and planned presentations, all with a coordinated communication program. They rallied not only ice users but many other community members as well. Most importantly, the ISF and their supporters attended every Lane County Commissioner meeting about the ice rink's future.

Through all their efforts and organization, many ISF members secretly wondered whether we were tilting at windmills. The county had a $10 million budget deficit, and the cost to repair the growing frost heave could be well over $2 million.

County and rink leadership agreed to temporarily close the rink to evaluate options in March 2010, once the Eugene Generals season had ended. When skaters and rink supporters first heard about the plan, many were shocked and expressed frustration to the Fair Board and County Commissioners.

Lane County citizens had mixed feelings. Most were generally supportive of the ice arena but concerned about the county's finances; others felt it was time for the rink to close. *The Register-Guard* letters to the editor and online comments were getting testy. The commentary traversed the emotional spectrum — passionate, humorous, angry, hopeful, resentful, and some were even flagged as offensive.

Soon after the rink closed, the fairgrounds demolished the building with the OSU Extension Service office. The rink could be next.

The controversy barreled toward the Lane County Commission's open meeting on July 7th, 2020, where they would decide whether to reopen the rink in the fall or close it forever. ISF was on its way to raising funds toward rink repairs, with $50,000 raised by July; its next milestone was raising $2.4 million by March 2011 for major repairs, as identified by a consultant hired by the county to assess the ice rink.

High anxiety filled the air in the packed room at the Lane County Public Service Building. As they watched the proceedings, hockey players, figure skaters, rink supporters, and young boys in their Junior Generals shirts were on pins and needles.

The Vote

There were three votes. The first vote was whether to close the rink. No more information was requested, and there would be no public testimony. It failed 3-2.

The crowd breathed a cautious sigh of relief as they lined up to testify in favor of the rink. No one testified to support the closure of the rink. However, fair manager Rick Reno sat at the commissioner's table and stated that an ice rink that doesn't break even belongs on the chopping block. Bill Dwyer added:

> If we can't close an ice rink that don't pay for itself, how are we going to make these cuts on women, infants and children? Where the hell is that going to come from?

The commissioners discussed increasing the user fees to generate more revenue from those who use the ice rink. Bill Fleenor was the swing vote. Rob Handy and Pete Sorenson wanted to see the rink continue, while Bill Dwyer and Faye Stewart, representing the more rural parts of the county, were solidly against it.

The second vote was to double the cost of all fees; if the usage continued at current levels, it would provide enough revenue. It failed 3-2 as well.

The air went out of the room. Someone started to cry. "Shit!" said another loudly enough to be heard by all. Jon Brand posted on Facebook:

> What a Commissioners Meeting! At about 11:15 am, they voted to shut the rink down, but Fleenor, Hardy, and Sorenson kept talking, pushing in the face of brutal opposition from Dwyer and Reno.

But the conversation continued. As the crowd watched in quiet desperation, the commissioners discussed the frost heave, maintenance costs, and alternatives for rink operations. Pete Sorenson jumped in with a motion to keep the rink open and triple the fees. He looked at Bill Fleenor, who said: "Let's give them a chance."

The motion passed with a 3-2 vote; the rink could reopen in the fall. Also, Faye Stewart softened his stance and was willing to listen to any reasonable proposal that could make the rink successful. The crowd was happy but a bit confused. Triple the fees?

The new fees were published soon after the meeting:

> $11.40 - Youth public session (previously $4)
> $18.75 - Adult public session ($5)

$10 - Skate rental ($3)

$61 - Freestyle cost per hour ($8)

$23 - Drop-in hockey cost per hour ($10)

$250 - Private rental cost per hour ($235)

$385 - Group lessons cost per person ($100)

$250 - Lane Amateur Hockey Association cost per hour ($212)

$250 - Oregon Ducks cost per hour ($200)

$250 - Eugene Generals cost per hour ($185)

One parent called the fees a cruel joke and noted that public skating for a family of four could cost $100.

In late September, the Eugene Generals began hockey practices, and LCI celebrated its grand reopening on October 3rd with clinics, exhibitions, music, and food. Skaters were thrilled to be on the ice again but uncertain about the rink's future.

The County Commission said the community had to raise $2.4 million by March to guarantee long-term rink improvements. By that time, ISI had raised just $63,000.

Then a miracle occurred.

THE RINK EXCHANGE

Ken Evans saved the day. He would later say:

> I'm an engineer by training, right? We say, What's the problem?
> What are the variables? How do you solve it? I like to tell it straight
> and have a problem to solve. I don't like to have all of this polit-
> ical stuff going on.

After the commissioner's vote, Ken began to work through the politics
behind the scenes to form a public-private partnership where he—through
his Hockey Oregon, LLC—could lease the rink from the county and run
the operation like a business.

As the owner of the Eugene Generals, Ken had a vested interest in keeping the ice rink open. In addition, Ken played in the adult hockey league and
would sometimes joke that he took on the rink just so he could continue to
play hockey. Of course, the endeavor was much more significant; fundamen-
tally, Ken wanted to give back to the community. It was not easy; he had to
mortgage his home to finalize the deal.

Ken developed a business plan and worked to convince Lane Events Center manager Rick Reno that Hockey Oregon could operate the rink and
meet all county requirements. The dasher boards' condition and potential
safety concerns were the most pressing issues. ISF had collected the necessary
funds to repair the boards, and Ken arranged to complete the work before

the September opening. The agreement with the county allowed Ken and his team to operate the facility independently. The building and land would remain public property, the operations would become a private venture, and Hockey Oregon would pay a monthly fee to the county. After reviewing the agreement and receiving positive input from Rick Reno, the County Commissioners unanimously approved the arrangement, knowing that the building would otherwise sit idle and be demolished without private support. The rink would be saved!

Newly named The Rink Exchange, the arena would continue to be the ice nexus between the public and the county. They announced that the rink would close every summer for three-to-four months when operating costs were highest, and usage waned. The summer closing allowed Hockey Oregon to attend to the years of deferred maintenance and to review changes to the concrete floor slab due to the existing frost heave. This approach improved rink facilities, and specialists determined that the frost heave had stabilized and would not pose a problem in the future.

The skating community breathed a sigh of relief as the transition to a public-private partnership began. However, the economic realities of the solution had vastly different impacts on the two main user groups. Hockey players were overjoyed. Although many would miss entering the cool rink for a game on a summer day, eight-to-nine months of hockey was vastly better than closing the rink forever. It takes little to get back into game rhythm, be it one month or a year away.

It was different for the figure skaters, who needed to skate year-round to excel. Returning to their spins and jumps after the summer break might take a few months. Club leadership knew the decision made sense financially, but the emotional response was devastating. Coaches left the program, high-level skaters stopped or tried other rinks, and the figure skating club was unsure of the future.

Fortunately, a new skating program came together quickly after much hard work and good fortune. Nine figure skaters enrolled at UO were able to coach immediately. The first Learn to Skate classes began in the fall of 2011, and the figure skating club was back in gear.

It was a new era for figure skaters, hockey players, and visitors at the Rink Exchange. Finally, the rink could operate independently, free of county politics and bureaucracy.

The rink survived, and the future looked bright!

30 Year Celebration (Photo courtesy of the Rink Exchange)

EPILOGUE

June 2023

The Rink Exchange keeps moving forward. Every Wednesday afternoon, once our senior pickup game is over, we gather on the bleachers above the rink, basking in our good fortunes and knowing how lucky we are to still be skating after all these years. We do what we do best: drink beer and tell tales.

One of the players is Ken Evans, president and owner of the Rink Exchange. He expects to continue operations at the fairgrounds, a location he believes is ideal. Ken and the dedicated team around him have managed to keep the rink operating through a myriad of challenges, including the recent COVID pandemic. The 2022-2023 season has been a good one. Public skating attendance was so strong that the rink had to turn people away numerous times and frequently ran out of rental skates. Ideally, Ken would like to add a second sheet of ice in the future.

Just before our hockey game, we often see figure skater Carolyn Brown and ice dancer Rex Betz wowing the public skating attendees with their expertise. The Eugene Figure Skating Club's membership has decreased since the heyday of the 1990s, but the organization remains strong and is an integral part of the Rink Exchange community.

Daniel Gomez coordinates the thriving hockey programs — youth teams, adult hockey leagues, and the popular Learn-to-Play Academy. Women continue to play a significant role in the rink's hockey activities. An increasing number of adult women athletes attend the Hockey Academy, and local players participated in Oregon's 2023 19U all-girls team led by two Lane County coaches, Justin Kern, former head coach of the Eugene Generals, and long-time Junior Generals coach, Dan Trent.

The rink closes in the summer, an understandable break that has been in place since the Rink Exchange took over operations. This year it will reopen in early September. Throughout the warm days of summer, skaters and hockey players anxiously look forward to getting back on the ice.

Chuck Selden (Photo courtesy of the Seldon family)

Time, like a jet plane, moves too fast. We are reminded of mortality as some older skaters pass on with increasing frequency. Earlier this year, Dick Fulwiler, a popular and respected adult hockey player, died at age 83. We learned in May that one of the original elders, Chuck Seldon, passed away. He was 94. When the family put together his obituary, they chose this photo of Chuck in his Oregon State Beavers socks, lacing up his hockey skates.

We all know we will need to hang up our skates for some reason or another, making our time on the ice even more special.

With each passing comes a new beginning, a new generation. Eddie LeRoy and Joel Dunham skated in the Wednesday hockey game in late May with their sons, EJ and Max. The kids were outstanding and smoothly zipped around a few old guys to make impressive plays. It did not matter how skilled they were; the fact that they were out there playing with their dads was enough. Every player felt it.

The rink will continue, a treasured building above a simple one-inch sheet of ice, ready for the next generation and beyond.

Joel Dunham, Max Dunham, EJ LeRoy, Eddie LeRoy (Photo David Baslaw)

APPRECIATION

Thank you to everyone who has played a role in bringing this book to life. It has been an incredible team effort, and I am immensely grateful to all those whose fingerprints are on these pages. If, by chance, someone has been unintentionally overlooked, please don't hesitate to reach out, and I will gladly make the appropriate revisions.

A big thank you to:

- LeeAnn Sheehan for her initial revisions, patience, love, and support

- My children, Emily, Nika, Connor, and Kerry, for tolerating my obsession with writing this book and for being who they are

- Travis Moran, and Steve Rodgers for professional editing and kind guidance

- Steve Kuhn for creative expertise and a wonderfully designed book

- Ali Ammar Naseem for outstanding photo editing

- My beta readers for their suggestions and heartfelt encouragement along the way: Steve Hertzberg, Steve Ives, Cindy Jensen, Elizabeth King, Keith McConnell, John Nero, and Michael Rooke-Ley

- Gracious interviewees and those who have willingly shared photos and memorabilia:

Adult Hockey Players:

- Dick Abraham, Tom Bahls, Dave Baslaw, Jen Bills, Tim Birr, Mitch Boriskin, Jon Brand, Bob Carolan, Jessica Duggan, Mike Duggan, Ken Evans, Ladia Filip, Ken Gibb, Tom Goodrie, Cindy Haskell, Rich Hicks, Dort Howery, Jon Hoyt, David Jensen, Mike Kehoe, Ron Kellett, Stan Kull, Eddie LeRoy, Dave Lester, Sid Magee, Julie Pfaff, Bill Poppie, Mary Reilly, John Rowell, Rich Salahor, Bob Schauer, Dan Schneiderhan, Wayne Shantz, Terry Smith, Kevin Swingdoff, Milan Vatovec, Bob Weir, and Chris Wherity

Ducks Hockey:

- Tim Birr, Brian Duggan, Earl Erb, Jeff Gibb, Scott McCallum, Mike Sobol, and Darin Varzali

Eugene Snowcats:

- Jason Bergey, Todd Carroll, Garrett Krause, and Bill McIntosh

Broomball:

- Lola Broomberg, Tom Carroll, Howard Newman, Tom Kochevar, Mark Marzullo, Amy Sierzega, and Lynda Taylor

Figure Skating:

- Amy Adams-Schauer, Carolyn Brown, Tonya Harding, Lauri Khodabandehloo, Keith Monfort, Peg Monfort, and Patsy Moser

Speed Skating:

- John Downen, Arnie Goodman, Barb Kull, Steven Lader, and Ben Strehle

Lane County Commissioners:

- Jerry Rust, and Pete Sorenson

Lane County Ice:

- Clint Barnts

Additional Assistance:

- Eugene Public Library, Allison Fischer-Olson and the Lane County Historical Society & Museum, Robert Joseph, Becky Kirsch, and the Lane Events Center, Peter MacLeod, Steven Saxe, Kit Sibert, and the University of Oregon Library

1990S FIGURE SKATERS

Blake Aaron	Stephanie Bustard	Minta Crafts
Allison Abraham	Erika Bulay	Brittany Craig
Nick Abraham	Michelle Cardill Johnson	Michelle Cypriano
Kenyon Acton	Leslie Carey	Sarah Danielson
Crystal Anderson	Tyee Carr	Sephera Danourand
Robyn Baker	David Carr	Amanda Demers
Charlene Bauman	Meagan Carr	Andrea Demers
Corinne Becker	Casey Dickenson	Angela Demers
Zach Bessett	Kacie Dickenson	Uri Harding
Meghan Birr	Jesse Dietrich	Shannon Hartley
Kellee Blanchard	Ryan Dobrowski	Molly Hinson
Ryan Blomberg	Ian Donahue	Holly Holbrook
Mandy Bollenbaugh	Kara Cauthon	Maghan Holst
Kimberly Bourne	Carolyn Chance	Lindsay Edens
Jeanette Brandner	Casia Chappell	Lisa Edens
Adriana Brandner	Nicole Chilton	Brandi Elting
Melena Bronson	Jameson Clark	Brandi Elting
Meghan Brown	Christine Clark	Risa Ericson
Jenny Bruce	Brian Clendenin	Brayden Ericson
Jessica Brustard	Rachel Colby	Lindsey Evans
Jordan Burbee	Amy Cooper	Heather Finke
Brooke Burbee	Tatiana Cordova	Hilary Flaherty
Jayson Burmark	Amanda Couch	Paige Flaherty

Shawn Flannery

Dustin Fletcher

Nicole Fowler

Sara Frank

Lanissa Fry

Merrilee Gilliland

Courtney Grant

Natalie Grant

Katelyn Greer

Sarah Guthu

Bethany Lilley

Kary Elly Lindsay

Tucker Locken-Dahl

Brandon Lorenz

Laurel Loughran

Gina Hoppe

Mikayla Hurwitz

Erin Iskra

Kelly Jackson

Martha Jones

Jeremya Keartes

Sarah Keartes

Emily Kersten

Megan King

Kelly Kirklin

Toby Kirklin

Crissy Kirklin

Amy Kitchel

Jennifer Kosydar

Amanda Knowles

Laura Knox

Farema Khodahbandehloo

Jeannine Lamar

Samara LaRochelle

Jamie Offord

Kelsey Osden

Jennifer Ouimet

Leslie Parisa

Rose Pergament

Kellee Loughran

Kim Loughran

Emily Loughran

Hawaii Marstas

Michelle Martanick

Christina Mattfield

Jennifer Mayer

Adrienne McNabb

Sara McPherson

Emily Monfort

Kallisse Montague

Amber Moser

Lindsey Moser

Alex Murphy

Leah Naylor-Watson

Emily Newman

Christina Newman

Ainsley Nilsen

Paige Nilson

Shannon Siegler

Sara Smith

Shane Smith

Mary Smith

Lindsay Smith

Jessica Peters

Jenni Peterson

Allison Petsch

Lindsey Reynolds

Kim Rhodes

Nori Rice

Emma Robinson

Miranda Rogers

Janae Rozar

Krista Russow

McKenzie Schafer

Gillian Schauer

Caitlin Schauer

Lindsay Schauer

Alayna Schawartz

Nicole Schick

Tyler Schoonhoven

Nichole Shepherd

Julia Sherwood

Deanna Smith

Kathleen Steers

Ashley Steed

Stephanie Steward

Erica Steingrobe

Heather Stitch

Heidi Straub

Kendra Sullivan

Casey Sullivan

Mark Sullivan

Sandy Sullivan

Natalie Swan

Michelle Thompson

Samantha Thurman

Kristalyn Tiahrt

Heidi Tunnel

Kiran Virani	Kim Walton	Teresa Whittier
Cassandra Vogel	Deanna Walton	Kelsey Wiechert
Sophia Yan	Julia Ward	Mary Williams
Shannon Young	Trina Wester	Becky Williams
Caleb Walden	Anna Whittier	Chelsea Willoughby
Tara Waldon	Mark Whittier	Brooke Willoughby

EFSC OFFICERS

1990

President: Carolyn Brown

Vice-President: Lynda Harding

Secretary: Joan Cobb

Treasurer: Karin Couch

Youth Rep: Martha Jones

1992-1995

President: Amy Adams-Schauer

Vice-President: Sherry Willoughby

Secretary: Carol Peters

Treasurer: Teri Benefiel

1996

President: John Petsch

Vice-President: Sandy Buch

Secretary: Beth Nayloer

Treasurer: Teri Benefiel

Board Member: Tyee Carr

Board Member: Sherry Willoughby

1990S HOCKEY TEAMS

LAHA Teams | 1990 WINTER and SUMMER

Incomplete Data

CASCADE MEDICAL

Bob Carolan	Dick Abraham	Steve Hamilton
Brandon Matz	Ed McNichol	Tom Ragland
Brant WojacK	Ron Kellett	Troy Prentice
Brian Walker	Scott Lindsay	

GOOD TIMES

Alan Dahlquist	John Grimes	Roger Hanson
Bruce Kelly	Ken Kerkhoff	Scott Griswold
Dan Derlacki	Paul Knobel	Wayne Shantz
Gary Flannery	Roberta Zais	

SHOOTERS PUB

Al French	Dave Koranda	Ken Hadlock
Bill Morris	David Jensen	Stan Kull
Bill Poppie	Dick Fulwiler	Ted Poole
Brad Copeland	Howard Newman	Terry Smith
Bryan Malakoff	John Burns	Tom Dreyer
Chuck Gottfried		

UNIVERSITY of OREGON

Scott Auerbach	Eric Latimer	Ron Polsky
Brad Paris	Lyle Grant	Scott Brown
Bryan Black	Mark Liebert	Stefan Bjarnason
Dan Baker	Mike McHugh	

TEAM ATHLETIC

Andy Fry	Dave Tisiot	Mike Cameron
Cam Cairney	Greg Gove	Sid Magee
Charles Salamone	John Femol	Steve Clark
Curtis Roney	Mike Berry	

PLAY IT AGAIN

Alex Schumacher	David Brooks	Josh Tuckman
Bob Carolan	Ed McNichol	Richard Staley
Bob Weir	Jane Merdinger	Steve Victor
Brian Clendenin	John O'Donnell	Tom Lerra

RANGERS

Alan Dahlquist	Dave Tisiot	Roger Hanson
Andy Fry	Mark Guyett	Tim Washburn
Brad Copeland	Paul Knobel	

ANGUS INN

Bob LaDouceur	Roger DuBuc	Thom Moore

1990-1991 WINTER

ANGUS INN

Alex Schumacher	Ken Hadlock	Ron Polsky
David Jensen	Mark Liebert	Ted Poole
Gary Flannery	Mike Sheehan	Thom Moore
Hector Smith	Ole Hansen	Tim Washburn
Jeff Cichosz	Richard Densmore	Tom Dreyer
John Meienhofer		

CASCADE MEDICAL

Bob Carolan	Dan Derlacki	Mike Stolz
Bob Schauer	Dick Abraham	Roberta Zais
Bob Weir	John Femol	Shane Peters
Brad Paris	Mike Berry	Steve Victor
Brian Walker	Mike Cameron	Troy Prentice
Curtis Roney		

GOOD TIMES

Alan Dahlquist	Mark Guyett	Scott Auerbach
Bruce Kelly	Paul Knobel	Scott Griswold
Ed McNichol	Roger DuBuc	Steve Hertzberg
John Grimes	Roger Hanson	Terry Smith
Ken Kerkhoff	Roger Lloyd	Wayne Shantz
Kevin Halchuk		

SHOOTERS PUB

Al French	Bryan Malakoff	Howard Newman
Bill Morris	Charles Salamone	John Burns
Bill Poppie	Chris Becker	John O'Donnell
Brad Copeland	Chuck Gottfried	Lyle Grant
Bryan Black	Dave Koranda	Stan Kull

TEAM ATHLETIC

Bob LaDouceur	Dick Fulwiler	Michael Kelly
Brad Zubeck	Greg Gove	Sid Magee
Cam Cairney	Joel Ehrlich	Stefan Bjarnason
Chris Chester	John Shannon	Steve Clark
Dave Tisiot	Lowell Nelson	Tom Bahls
David Brooks		

UNIVERSITY of OREGON

Andy Fry	Darin Varzali	Mike McHugh
Ben Bartscht	Eric Latimer	Ryan Green
Brian Clendenin	Josh Tuckman	Scott Brown
Damian Jergensen	Kevin Walchuk	Steve Hamilton
Dan Baker	Mike Accord	Tom Lerra

1991-1992 WINTER

6TH STREET GRILL

John Burns ©	Greg Gore	Mike Sheehan
Alex Schumacher	John Shannon	Steve Clark
Bryan Black	Kevin Halchuk	Steve Hertzberg
Chuck Gottfried	Michael Cameron	Tim Washburn
Curtis Roney		

CASCADE MEDICAL

Bob Carolan ©	Dick Abraham	Roger Lloyd
Al French	Dick Fulwiler	Shad Hayden
Bob Schauer	Karissa Weeks	Stan Baldwin
Dan LaPoma	Kim Mattson	Stan Kull
David Jensen	Rich Hicks	

GOOD TIMES

Bob Weir ©	John O'Donnell	Ron Silver
Bill Poppie	Lowell Nelson	Steve Sisson
Cam Cairney	Mike Duggan	Terry Smith
Dave Koranda	Randy Lieberman	Troy Prentice
Jens Mullen	Randy Teal	

NEW OREGON MOTEL

Dan Derlacki ©	Eric Latimer	Steve Victor
Anthony Ottman	Lyle Grant	Tom Bahls
Antony Cooper	Ole Hansen	Tom Dreyer
Bill Morris	Ron Rennick	Wayne Shantz
Craig Brusegaard		

TEAM ATHLETIC

Andy Fry ©	Jo Gibson	Ryan Greene
Dave Tisiot	John Femal	Sid Magee
David Brooks	Mike Berry	Steve Hamilton
Don Harker	Richard Densmore	Tom Ponce
Hector Smith		

LAHA FLYERS

Ted Poole ©	Jeff Sorenson	Paul Knobel
Bob LaDouceur	Ken Hadlock	Roger Hanson
Doug Sanderson	Laura Harper	Scott Griswold
Gary Spinrad	Mitch Boriskin	Sean Schoppe
Gordy Longhurst		

1992 SUMMER

6th STREET GRILL

John Burns ©	John Rowell	Scott Klemick
Alex Schumacher	Mike Duggan	Steve Hertzberg
Bob Schauer	Ole Hansen	Steve Victor
David Bergstrom	Rich Hicks	Tom Dreyer
Doug Sanderson	Scott Griswold	

CASCADE MEDICAL

Bob Carolan ©	Jody Proctor	Ron Rennick
Bill Poppie	Lyle Grant	Terry Smith
Dick Abraham	Mike Sheehan	Tim Birr
Hector Smith	Mike Ahten	Tracy Owens
John O'Donnell	Roger Hanson	

TEAM ATHLETIC

Andy Fry ©	Laura Harper	Stan Kull
Alan Dahlquist	Michael Cameron	Steve Clark
Chuck Gottfried	Paul Knobel	Tim Washburn
Dave Koranda	Shane Jensen	Timothy Foster
Gary Flannery	Sid Magee	

LAHA FLYERS

Ted Poole ©	John Harper	Stan Baldwin
Al French	Kevin Swingdoff	Tom Martin
Bob LaDouceur	Michael Seestadt	Troy Prentice
Curtis Roney	Mitch Boriskin	Wayne Shantz
Jeff Cichosz	Randy Stefanson	

1994-1995 WINTER

MAPLE LEAFS

Bob Carolan ©	Jeff Cichosz	Mitch Boriskin
Bob LaDouceur	John Shannon	Neal Duttlinger
Darryl Scheck	Jonathan Brooks	Shad Hayden
Flint Doungchak	Mike Duggan	Stan Siemens
Hector Smith		

KINGS

Craig Brusegaard ©	Jacques de Staint Phalle	Mason Saxton
Al French	John Mahon	Ron Rennick
Alan Dahlquist	John Trajlinek	Shane Hegarty
Charlie Janz	Kevin Vergin	Tim Freemark
Galan Ohmart		

BLACKHAWKS

Bob Weir ©	Jody Proctor	Sid Magee
Barclay Brasted	John Capell	Stan Baldwin
Cory Vance	John Kelly	Tim Washburn
Don Derlacki	Kevin Swingdoff	Wayne Shantz
Jeff Winchester	Paul Knobel	

SHARKS

Steve Twohig ©	Dick Abraham	Rich Hicks
Alex Schumacher	John Burns	Rich Nellis
Antony Cooper	John Rowell	Seth Prouser
Bob Schauer	Mike Ahten	Tom Bascom
Chuck Gottfried	Ole Hansen	

H.C.K.

Stan Kull ©	Gary Flannery	Ted Poole
Bryan Malakoff	Greg Merchep	Tom Dreyer
Chris Rossi	Jim Herdegen	Troy Prentice
Dale Romanko	Laura Harper	Will Brown
Dave Lester	Steve Hertzberg	

1995 SUMMER

MAPLE LEAFS

Bob Carolan ©	Darryl Scheck	Michael Seestadt
Al French	Greg Baker	Mitch Boriskin
Chuck Gottfried	Jacques de Staint Phalle	Richard Nellis
Dan LaPoma	John Mahon	Tom Goodrie
Danny Sullivan	Kevin Carolan	Troy Prentice

BLACKHAWKS

Bob Weir ©	Dave Ewers	Kevin Vergin
Alan Dahliquist	Dick Fulwiler	Laura Harper
Bunk Keggan	J.T. Mackey	Roberta Zais
Chuck Selden	John Capell	Tim Freemark
Colin Sorhus	Jon Hoyt	

SHARKS

John Burns ©	Eric Olsen	Mark Guyett
Anthony Hazenfield	Flint Doungchak	Stan Siemans
Barclay Brasted	Galen Ohmart	Ted Poole
Chris Rossi	Jody Proctor	Tim Birr
Dave Lester	Larry McMullen	

H.C.K.

Stan Kull ©	Kevin Swingdoff	Paul Knobel
David Jensen	Mason Saxton	Sid Magee
Dick Abraham	Matthew Mieding	Terry Smith
Hector Smith	Mike Duggan	Tim Washburn
Jim Herdegan	Mike Sheehan	Wayne Shantz

1998 SUMMER

MAPLE LEAFS

Larry McMullen ©	Eddie LeRoy	Mitch Boriskin
Bob Weir	Flint Doungchak	Peter McGregor
Brian Raygor	Jared Ritzer	Tom Alexander
Charlie Janz	Keri Sanchez	Tyler Shaffar
Dave Koranda	Mike Sheehan	

KINGS

Shane Hegarty ©	David Stark	Paul Knobel
Bill Poppie	Joey Chandler	Steve Hertzberg
Bob Carolan	Jonathan Brooks	Tim Esty
Bob Schauer	Lyle Laver	Uri Harding
Chuck Selden	Miah Corcoran	William Holburn

BLACKHAWKS

Ted Poole ©	John Rowell	Robyn Perry
Al French	Mike DiBitetto	Ron Colby
Ben Williams	Phil Squire	Sean Sahoppe
Jeff Cichosz	Randy Anderson	Tim Washburn
John Capell	Richard Nellis	Tom Exley

SHARKS

Dave Lester ©	Dave Hoist	Kevin Swingdoff
Chris Cebra	Jacques de Staint Phalle	Rob Chasen
Craig Vieth	Jeff Ortiz	Steve Chaney
Dan LaPoma	Jim Herdegan	Wes Clay
Dave Ewers	John Walsh	

BLUES

Troy Prentice ©	Dick Fulwiler	Mike Gettinger
Bob Ladouceur	Hector Smith	Ron Kellett
Chris Olivares	John Dowell	Ryan Walsh
Curtis Roney	John Trajlinek	Terry Smith
Dennis Hamel	Jon Hoyt	

H.C.K.

Stan Kull ©	Kevin Vergin	Sid Magee
Barclay Brasted	Luigi Meneghelli	Tom Goodrie
Colin Sorus	Mark Hams	Vic Steuber
Dan Schneiderhan	Mike Duggan	Wayne Shantz
Dick Abraham	Phil Johnson	

1998-1999 WINTER

SHARKS

Larry McMullen ©	Mark Livingston	Suzanne Fisher
Al French	Mike DiBitetto	Tim Esty
Bob Dugre	Rich Nellis	Tim Washburn
Charlie Janz	Robyn Perry	Vic Steuber
Doug Washburn	Steve Hertzberg	

KINGS

Shane Hegarty ©	Jeff Ortiz	Randy Anderson
Bob Carolan	John Capell	Shad Hayden
Dan LaPoma	Jon Hoyt	Tom Alexander
Dan Schneiderhan	Lyle Laver	Tom Heer
Geoff Norman	Peter McGregor	

BLACKHAWKS

Ted Poole ©	Jacques de Staint Phalle	John Lucachick
Barclay Brasted	Jason Lee	Jonathan Brooks
Blaine Machart	Jeff Cichosz	Mike Duggan
Bob Weir	Jeff Landfried	Mike Sheehan
Hector Smith		

MAPLE LEAFS

Dave Lester ©	Ken Hadlock	Miah Corcoran
Brian Raygor	Keri Raygor	Phil Squire
Colin Sorus	Kevin Swingdoff	Sid Magee
Galen Ohmart	Kevin Vergin	Wes Clay
Joey Chandler	Luigi Meneghelli	

BLUES

Troy Prentice ©	Jared Ritzer	Paul Knobel
Chuck Selden	John Dowell	Phil Escanlar
Dave Tisiot	John Trajlinek	Ralph Corliss
Derek Miller	Josh Tuckman	Sean Sahoppe
Flint Doungchak	Mark Hams	Steve Chaney

H.C.K.

Stan Kull ©	John Walsh	Ryan Walsh
Anthony Bucher	Matt Cox	Terry Smith
Bob Schauer	Mitch Boriskin	Wayne Shantz
Dick Abraham	Ron Colby	Whitney Grumhaus
Jim Herdegan	Ron Kellett	

1999-2000 WINTER

SHARKS

Larry McMullen ©	Jonathan Brooks	Phil Squire
Bob Blair	Mark Hams	Tom Alexander
Darren Dunbar	Mike Duggan	Tommy Williams
Dave Ewers	Phil Escanlar	Troy Prentice
Galen Ohmart	Phil Johnson	

KINGS

Bob Carolan ©	Don Derlacki	John Capell
Andy Simpson	Doug Heer	John Lucachick
Bob Schauer	Jacob Kenworthy	Kevin Swingdoff
Chuck Selden	Jacques de Staint Phalle	Mitch Boriskin
Dick Fulwiler	Jeff Cichosz	Randy Anderson

BLACKHAWKS

Charlie Janz ©	John Rowell	Rob Gilkerson
Al French	John Trajlinek	Robyn Perry
Dave Koranda	John Walsh	Tom Goodrie
David Pierce	Kevin Vergin	Wayne Shantz
Jeff Landfried	Peter McGregor	

MAPLE LEAFS

Dave Lester ©	Geoff Norman	Shane Hegarty
Dan Schneiderhan	John Dowell	Steve Hertzberg
David Jensen	Michael VanPelt	Tim Esty
Dick Abraham	Mike Sheehan	Vic Steuber
Eric Koch	Rich Nellis	

RENEGADES

Tim Washburn ©	Jim Herdegan	Ron Colby
Barclay Brasted	Jon Hoyt	Ryan Herdegan
Bob Weir	Keri Raygor	Shad Hayden
Brian Raygor	Lance Bass	Sid Magee
Jeff Ortiz	Matt Cox	

H.C.K.

Stan Kull ©	John Grimes	Ted Poole
Anthony Bucher	Mike DiBitetto	Tom Heer
Chris Cebra	Paul Wanke	Walker Mallison
Hector Smith	Patrick Curran	Yates Exley
Joey Chandler	Ron Kellett	

2000-SUMMER

KINGS

Tom Goodrie ©	Jeff Ortiz	Phil Johnson
Chuck Selden	Joey Chandler	Robyn Perry
Dan Schneiderhan	Jonathan Brooks	Sid Magee
Dick Abraham	Matt Cox	Wayne Shantz
Galen Ohmart	Mike Duggan	

BLACKHAWKS

Charlie Janz ©	John Dowell	Phil Squire
Al French	John Trajlinek	Tamra Fowler
Andy Simpson	Larry McMullen	Terry Smith
Dennis Hamel	Mike Sheehan	Tim Esty
John Capell	Mitch Boriskin	

MAPLE LEAFS

Dave Lester ©	Jim Hurdoon	Ryan Herdegan
Barclay Brasted	John Grimes	Steve Hertzberg
Bob Weir	John Walsh	Tesha Torguson
Hector Smith	Mark Hams	Tom Alexander
Jacques de Staint Phalle	Rob Starkey	

H.C.K.

Stan Kull ©	Kevin Swingdoff	Rita Ann Monde
Bob Carolan	Michael VanPelt	Ron Kellett
Bob Schauer	Mike DiBitetto	Shannon Scott
David Pierce	Qutaidah Hamadah	Stacie Johnson
Jon Hoyt	Randy Anderson	Tyler Shaffar

LAHA OFFICERS

1990

President: Steve Hertzberg

Vice President: Roger Wherity

Secretary: Craig Brusegaard

Treasurer: Cathi Staley

Referee-in-Chief: Jeff Balough

1993

Commissioner: Steve Hertzberg

Treasurer: Mike Duggan

Referee-in-Chief: Jeff Balough

Scorekeeper: Vicki Van Artsdalen

1990-1991 Ducks Hockey

Player	Hometown
Mike Acord	Lapeer, MI
Scott Auerbach	Irvine, CA
Tom Bahls	Lexington, MA
Dan Baker	Omaha, NE
Ben Bartscht	Ann Arbor, MI
Scott Brown	Foster, RI
Chris Hoffman	Wellesley, MA
Todd Holthe	Minnetonka, MN
Damian Jorgensen	Grafton, ND
Ron Kellett	Winnipeg, Man
Tom Lerra	Boston, MA
Mark Liebert	Portland, OR
Mike McHugh	Salt Lake City, UT
Darin Varzali	Portland, OR
Ned White	Boston, MA

Head Coach: Mike Sobol

Trainer: Jill Walker

Power Skating: Vance Kirklin

Goalie Coach: Shane Peters

1995 Snowcats

Player Name	Hometown
Jason Beaton	Port Hawkesbury, NS
Bert Belvedere	Toronto, ONT
Jason Bergey	Chadds Ford, PA
Todd Carroll	North Haven, CT
John Copley	Inverness, NS
Eric Danielson	Coventry, RI
Brett Dunleavy	Charlotte, NC
Don Gagne	Bathurst, NB
Karel Hamr	Litomerice, Czech Rep
David Hebky	Brno, Czech Rep.
Kelly Hrycun	Edmonton, AL
Scott Humphrey	New Westminster, BC
Roman Kobrc	Teokuce, Czech Rep
Bill McIntosh	Duxbury, MA
Bill Morra	Toronto, ONT
Darren Naylor	White Rock, BC
Ryan Tansy	Spokane, WA
Brian Trenholm	Port Hood, NS
Kurt Walsten	Kenora, ONT
Darren Webb	Langley, BC
Lance Wolgemuth	Lancaster, PA

EUGENE, OREGON

by Dolly Parton

Eugene, Oregon, I'll remember you for the rest of my life
I won't forget how good you were to me.
No, and I won't be forgettin' all the kindness that you show.
To a homesick country girl a long, long way from Tennessee

Tired and weary and feelin' low
Among strange people, I didn't know.
A long, long way from home and a long time gone.
Oh, but Eugene, Oregon, you were kind.
The love you gave was genuine.
You gave me inspiration and the strength to carry on

Eugene, Oregon, I'll remember you for the rest of my life
And I won't forget how good you were to me.
Oh, an' I won't be forgettin' all the kindness that you show.
To a homesick country girl a long, long way from Tennessee

Oh, Eugene, Oregon, I have been trying to find a way to say thanks again
For standing up for me when I was alone
Oh, and I couldn't think of a better way.
To say the things that I wanted to say.
Then to take my old guitar, sit right down and write you a song

Eugene, Oregon, I'll remember you for the rest of my life
I won't forget how good you were to me.
No, and I won't be forgettin' all the kindness that you show.
To a homesick country girl a long, long way from Tennessee

The love you gave was genuine
Eugene, Oregon, I'll remember you for the rest of my life.

DOLLY PARTON,
Lane County Fairgrounds - 1972

JODY PROCTER MEMORIAL

Written by Sid Magee

There's a bunch of us here who played hockey with Jody. We want to honor him, our friend. And I have wondered what to say. I wish I could do Jack Kennedy as well as Jody could—just thinking about that makes me smile. But no one could.

I'd like to recount anecdotes from his life, but I haven't been a lifelong friend, so I don't know those stories. I do know there'd be a bookful of capers, romance, gaffs, and adventure. And that got me to thinking how amazing life is—and how amazing Jody's had to have been.

Just think of it. We come out of nowhere, running one leg of this timeless evolutionary relay race, and then we pass our genetic baton to the next generation, and seem to disappear. But the richness of that short lap is a miracle.

Count the special experiences of just one day: Like the freshness of dawn, watching a wild animal, interacting with different people, framing a house, scoring a goal, family meal, writing, working up a sweat, singing on the road, an ice cream cone, clean sheets, the smell of hay. And these aren't even the big ones. Like your first good kiss. Like seeing your kid graduate. Like feeling loved.

I figure, if you experience only four things a day, in 55 years that's 80,000 life events! Can you imagine the 80,000 events in the stage play Life of Jody? It makes me blush to even contemplate—and I'm sure he wasn't limited to 4 a day. Can you imagine all the different changes of scenery, acts, and actors that filled that Life of Jody stage? What an amazing and wonderful play it was. We were all lucky to have had parts in it. And it's closing to a packed house.

So, I think we should not mourn the fact that Jody's not here; but remember ...

Marvel and celebrate the wonderful fact that he was here.

We only knew Jody on the ice, on the bus to the Old Timers' Tournament, and in the locker room. But that was all we needed to know ... to love the guy. He skated with heart. He never said a mean word. And in the locker room, Jody didn't talk about hockey; he talked about literature! To the end, he cared about all of us ... and was a truly gentle man.

We celebrate Jody—who's still alive in the hearts of everyone who loved him in the natures of his lovely kids   in the things he wrote - like a star that's stopped burning, whose light we can still see. And that's amazing.

My God you had a lot of friends, Jody. But you hugged us and slipped away.

We're gonna be skating a man short, but we won't forget you, Jody.

THE WRECK OF THE OLD CURTIS RONEY

Written by Sid Magee

Lane Ice it is said never gives up its dead
from the big rink they call Passitome.
But the Zam can't erase
all the blood from the place
from The Wreck of the Old Curtis Roney.

One Old-Timers night by the dawn's early light
we were skating like no one could hurt us. When somebody let rip,
"Abandon the ship!
and clear the ice, cause here comes Curtis!"

He had circled the ice first once, and then twice,
exuding aerobic condition, when he started to wheeze, like the Exxon Valdez
or some bad LSD apparition.

Then this gigantic ghost headed out coast to coast
with the puck and the smile of a lecher. And forecheckers, they say,
that got in his way
ended up on the boards or a stretcher.

Only Dan stood between that momentous machine
and the fate of our valiant goaltender, when across the P.A.
Bruce Springsteen did say,
"..no retreat, Baby, and no surrender."

We back skated with dread when he traversed the red,
taunting, "Boys, I've got something to show ya."
As he came down the rink, Tim Birr, tightening his sphincter,
cried, "Fellas, it's been good to know ya."

You won't live, so they say, if you get in the way
of big Curtis, now that he is older.
But Dan hadn't been taught to dread juggernauts,
so he lowered his unpadded shoulder.
On Curtis bore down,
topping three hundred pound,
on a defense big as Mickey Rooney. But LaPoma's election,
to do a C-section,
just let the air out of Old Roney.

At nine thirty-five not a man was alive
who had flattened this upright piano. At a quarter to ten,
when the giant caved in,
the chant was struck up, "Book 'em Dan-O!"

There were whimpers and moans from that big bag of bones,
and transfusion was called for by many. But "Let's play!" someone said,
so we left him for dead,
and a tow truck was called for by Danny.

Curtis lay on his ass looking like Mama Cass
or a whale that got beached on the ice pack.
Then he limped to the bench with its horrible stench
and said, "What I need is an icepack."

And what of our Dan, the bandaging man,
as he rose from his heroic run-in?
Did he wish that he'd had on full shoulder pads,
some mace, or maybe a cannon?
"Just a word of advice",
Dan said, leaving the ice
after Curtis assumed the position;
"When you skate cross that line your asses are mine,
and they'd best be insured for collision."

Oh, the worst you could think is to be on the rink
in the path of a charging Zamboni.
But the smarter advice is, "Stay off the ice!"
if the runaway freight's Curtis Roney.

You will hear people talk of Jack and the Stalk
or Goliath and David, the bony; but the Oregon Trail
tells of no greater tale
than Dan's wrecking of big Curtis Roney.

Balladeers, they may sing of the Hobbit and Ring,
of Liberty Valence, and Jonah. But the legend lives on,
in poem and song,
of the man that they call Dan LaPoma.

REFERENCES

Chill Factor, how a minor league hockey team changed a city forever by David Patterson and Greg Hertz, and Bob Hunter copyright 2015 Sports Publishing, Delaware

Corvallis Gazette-Time, selected articles — 1949

Eugene 1945–2000 Decisions That Made a Community by The City Club of Eugene copyright 2000 Xlibris Corporation

Eugene's Civic Stadium by Joe R Blakely 2009, First edition Crane Dance Publications

Eugene Modernism 1935–1965 — Historic Preservation Northwest — 1991

The Register-Guard, selected articles 1940–2022

Eugene Weekly, selected articles — 2010

Fruit of the Sixties, The founding of the Oregon Country Fair by Suzi Prozanski copyright 2009 Coincidental Communications Eugene, Oregon

Home Ice, Reflections on Backyard Rinks and Frozen Ponds by Jack Falla copyright 2000 McGregor Publishing, Tampa, Florida

Lane County Historian, selected articles — 1991

Lane County Historical Society & Museum Oral History Program — Interview Subject: Eugene Thiessen

Late in the Third, Observations from Both Sides of the Glass by Joe Bertagna copyright 2021 Daily Printing, Beverly Farms, Massachusetts

Lonely Girl, Gracious God by Lauri Khodabandehloo copyright 2011 Deep River Books, Sisters, Oregon

Milwaukee Journal Sentinel, selected articles — 1998

Oregon Blue Book 2019 by the Office of the Secretary of State copyright 2019 Sheridan Books, Ann Arbor, Michigan

Oregon Daily Emerald, selected articles 1990–2010

Salem Statesman Journal, selected articles — 1949

Spokane Spokesman-Review, selected articles — 1995

The Rink: Stories from Hockey's Home Towns, Chris Cuthbert and Scott Russell, copyright 1957 Penguin Group, Toronto, Ontario

Snowcats

https://www.hockeydb.com/ihdb/stats/leagues/150.html

https://medium.com/@garrett_krause/las-vegas-hockey-history-18a788febfa1

Broomball

https://www.youtube.com/watch?v=fLFW0wMMu8I

EARLY REVIEWS

Rink: Stories from an Oregon Ice Arena is a delight. A warm-hearted look at a cool community facility, this book entertained and informed me from start-to-finish. Featuring insider stories, photos, and well-researched history, *Rink*, like the ice arena, is a Lane County treasure.

Elizabeth K. Gerlach,
Author of Autism Treatment Guide

Rink is an informative, historical, and thoroughly entertaining portrait of a simple building and the hundreds who have skated through it. You don't have to understand hockey or be able to skate backward to enjoy this book. If you are passionate about skating at all, it is a must-read. Pick up hockey games. Ice skating families. Olympic stars. Professional hockey teams. Skating through disability, And much more.

John Nero,
Journalist, Author

Both lighthearted and factually accurate. Mike's love of this rink—and that of all those about whom he writes—shines through on every page.

Steve Hertzberg,
first President Lane Amateur Hockey Association

Rink brought me back to a time I had literally skated away from and opened the floodgates of ice rink memories. It is an uplifting, heartwarming and often amusing account of the life of an ice rink, those who worked there, and those who skated its sheet of ice. It is a story of hockey players, figure skaters, broomballers, speed skaters, supporters, public recreators and the greater community who enjoyed the games and ice shows.

Sheehan's book recounts the determination of an eclectic mix of ice enthusiasts to develop and operate an ice rink against a myriad of odds. This story of persistence is a metaphor for the most essential life skill learned in skating. When we fall, we get up. One does not have to be a skating enthusiast to appreciate this story of an ice rink. It is a delightful and inspiring account of a unique community and their ability to get up again and again.

Cindy Jensen,
Retired Lane Ice Center Skating Director and Arena Manager

I highly recommend Michal Sheehan's *Rink*. Michael's narrative is both informative and entertaining. I never played hockey or skated for fun, yet I was immediately taken in by the warm, personal stories included in his account of the Rink. Michael gives the participants a voice. He lets them tell their stories. And their stories are fascinating. Rink is a piece of the puzzle that is the history of Lane County.

Steve Ives, *Author*

Rink, a rich and diverse history of Lane County's ice arena, is vividly brought to life through a series of captivating tales and personal accounts. The reader is ushered to a coveted front-row seat for this intimate and often amusing glimpse into a resilient community of warm-hearted enthusiasts who refused to give up on a dream.

Curtis Anderson,
former Register-Guard sports journalist

In *Rink*, Michael Sheehan has thoroughly researched and colorfully described the fascinating history of an ice skating rink in a mid-sized, Oregon city. Like skating itself, the book is smooth flowing yet interspersed with the unexpected including numerous, witty anecdotes. Readers, whether skaters or not, will enjoy hearing about the many challenges of creating and caring for this unique community gem—its rink. Skate on!

Keith McConnell, PhD
Lifelong hockey player

ABOUT THE AUTHOR

F. Michael, "Mike" Sheehan grew up in Melrose, Massachusetts, skating on the frozen Ell Pond each winter.

His most memorable hockey moment is watching Bobby Orr fly through the air with his stick raised after scoring his famous 1970 overtime goal at the Boston Garden. Mike jumped over the boards as Captain John Bucyk skated by with the Stanley Cup, slipped, and knocked Johnny McKenzie to the ice with a cut block. The following day, he appeared on page three of the *Boston Herald* in a photo celebrating from the back of Pascal Fusco's VW convertible.

He moved to Eugene in 1972, attending the University of Oregon and playing on the UO club soccer team. He spent the next decade traveling and working across North America and Europe.

Mike has played in the Lane County Adult hockey league for over 30 years and joined the Oregon Old Growth team for the 2023 Snoopy Senior Tournament's over-70 division.

He lives with his wife, LeeAnn, in Eugene, Oregon. They have four adult children: Emily, Nika, Connor, and Kerry. Michael, LeeAnn, and their dog Sierra frequently travel in their converted campervan throughout the West.

This is his first book.

Rink (Photo courtesy of The Rink Exchange)